Dear
Pat Cooper,

FIRST EDITION

ISBN # 978-0-615-31877-6
AUTHOR: Michael Caputo
Copyright © 2006
EDITOR: Frank Baldassare
COVER CONCEPT & PHOTO RETOUCHING: Carol Caputo
BOOK DESIGN: Sandra L. Baker
INTERIOR PAGE LAYOUT: rubberband graphics, inc.,
www.rubberbandgraphics.com
PUBLISHED BY: Cody Boy Books
a subsidiary of Cody Boy Inc., www.codyboyentertainment.com

.....This book is dedicated to the two women in my life who have always been there:

- My mother, Dolores Nola DePaci, for her love, strength, and unwavering belief in me.

- And in loving memory of my paternal grandmother, Louise Caputo, who gave me a lifetime of great memories and gave my father a lifetime of great material.

Mom

Grandma

CONTENTS

ACKNOWLEDGEMENTS

... First, I want to thank my Aunt Carol for all her support, creative inspiration and guidance. I am forever grateful to her for all the time and much-needed feedback she graciously contributed to my project.

... Second, I want to thank my mother for her inextinguishable love and her faith in my writing.

... Third, I want to thank my good friend Frank Baldassare for editing and structuring my work while being so respectful of my voice. Thank you for your dedication, friendship, and relentless effort to get this book off the ground.

... A special thanks to Howard Stern and the Infinity Broadcasting team for giving me the forum and all that air time to speak my mind. I am forever indebted to you guys for making my first father and son talk possible and bringing this all to the forefront.

... Many thanks to CBS Studios and Tribune Entertainment, especially my ex-boss, Geraldo Rivera. It was an honor and a privilege to be part of that team. A big thanks to the producers for allowing me to tell my story on national television.

... Thank you Joan Rivers for having Howard Stern and Angela Bowie on your show at the same time. That special combination gave me the opportunity to prove myself and ultimately got me hired.

... Thank you David Bowie and Mick Jagger for your unique friendship.

... And last, but not least, I want to thank my late friend Bill. If it wasn't for his phone call I would have never called the Howard Stern radio show and none of this would have ever happened. I miss you Bill. May your soul rest in peace.

Dear Pat Cooper,

Michael Caputo

CODY BOY
BOOKS

Published by CODY BOY BOOKS
a subsidiary of Cody Boy Inc., NEW YORK.
www.codyboyentertainment.com
2009

Preface

It seems like I have been writing this book most of my life. Like most kids that come from divorced parents I thought it was my fault. (I was a nervous and demanding kid that could drive anyone crazy) But what did I do? What did any of us do to make my father keep away from the whole family and go find himself a new one?

At first I wanted to write about how much I hated my father for not caring about me and my sister, but deep down all I wanted was an opportunity to tell him how much I loved him and missed him being in my life. I tried my best to tell my father about my life, but he never heard me. Every time we met he found fault with my clothes, my manners, and always...always the rest of the family. He hated us with every fiber of his being and I could never understand why. These attacks became part of his routine and a way of not getting too close to me or anyone else in our family. It was a wall too high for me to climb. It never failed; no matter how many times I tried to connect with my father, Pasquale Caputo, all I ever got from him was Pat Cooper the angry comedian.

Chapter One

Dear Pat Cooper,

The first time I met Pat Cooper I was five years old. My mother had taken my sister and I to a small neighborhood playground in Park Slope, Brooklyn. I was running around pretending to be an airplane, my arms fully extended noisily circling the sliding pond when my mother called out, "Michael get over here!" I stood there defiantly with my arms folded just looking at her. "Right now!" she demanded. She sounded serious so I ran to her side. She reached for my hand as she focused on the two men that were entering the playground. My mother explained that the tall one with the glasses was my father and the other man was his lawyer. I didn't even know what a lawyer was but I did understand that I was about to meet my dad. My whole body trembled with excitement.

I thought as soon as my father saw me he would lift me up off the ground and give me the biggest hug ever, just like I used to see my friends' fathers do with them all the time. Instead I got a tap on the head and a half smile. I was heartbroken; even the lawyer sensed it. The lawyer tried his best to break the awkward moment by trying to shake my hand. I had my eyes glued to my father who just stood there the whole time with an annoyed look on his face. It was obvious that he didn't want to be there. He didn't say a word to my sister and I, and he completely ignored my mother. The lawyer did all the talking which made me more uncomfortable and I started biting my nails. When my mother saw that she grabbed my fingers from my mouth and held onto my hand with her usual firm grip. Then she told me to go play on the sliding pond. The moment she let go of my hand I ran over to the big slide and climbed up the ladder. I stood at the top for a few seconds patiently waiting to see if I could get my father's attention.

"Daddy look," I said as I leaned forward and made my descent. When my feet hit the ground I just stood there a minute embracing my achievement and hoping he would ask me to do it again. Then I realized he had missed the whole thing. He was too busy talking with his lawyer. I heard the lawyer call him Mr. Cooper. Nobody ever told me that my father had a different last name than me—not even Grandma Caputo. And she was the one that knew everything about him. After all she was his mother.

I hurried back up the ladder again. At the top, I could see my mother and my sister watching intently, but he wasn't even looking in my direction. I don't know where it came from but I shouted "Mr. Cooper," and waved my hand at him as I came down the slide. When I hit the bottom I looked up and he was standing over me like a tree. I smiled at him thinking that I had finally gotten his attention. He looked at me then turned around and mumbled something to his lawyer. The next thing I knew we were in a car on our way home. I don't remember ever leaving the playground so abruptly. I sat silently in the backseat clinging to my mother. I thought I'd done something wrong. That day set the stage for the next 35 years.

I lived on the second floor in Grandma's three-family brownstone with my mother and sister for the first ten years of my life. Even though she lived downstairs from us, her apartment was an extension of ours. We never had to knock, either. In those ten years, my father never once stopped by to see us, and I don't remember ever seeing him downstairs at grandmas, either. My grandmother's dining room table was the place where I parked myself almost every night. I could always count on her for a hearty meal and a good laugh. Whenever we were alone usually enjoying a dish of macaroni she'd turn to me and say, "You wanna listen to your father's records?" Then she'd start elaborating on his material, sometimes for hours, talking about the family, her youth, and the good old days growing up in Brooklyn. She had the most incredible stories and it usually turned out that her version was funnier than his.

Just to set the record straight: my father learned the art of entertaining from my grandmother. She had a quick wit and was the ultimate hostess. Her kitchen was her stage!

My grandmother did her best to make sure that I got to know my father through the wonderful stories she would tell me about him. She encouraged me to love him and was the one who gave me hope about one day having a relationship with him. If it wasn't for her I wouldn't have known anything about him. She showed me another side of her son Pasquale Caputo: a side that I could love. A side that was very different from the man Pat Cooper who I had met in the playground. I couldn't rely on my mother doing any of that because she was too busy trying to keep everything together. I couldn't rely on my grandfather either because he was never around. My grandparents got separated before I was born. I'm lucky if I saw my grandfather five times in my life—the fifth time being in the funeral parlor when he was laid out. I would later come to understand that he had the same wall up my father had.

I always knew there was a situation between my father and the family, but nobody ever said a word to me about it or explained anything to me; at least not until I got older. In those days adults didn't discuss their problems with the children. My mother and grandmother sheltered me from all the ugly stuff as much and as long as they could. I had a wonderful childhood and I can thank my mother and grandmother for that. They saturated me with love and always had all the bases covered.

My grandmother was thrown into the job of caretaker at a very young age which would continue into her adult life. She was the matriarch, the pulse, and the one that held everybody together. She was born in Brooklyn, New York on All Saints Day, November 1st, 1907. She was the third child born out of nine. Her parents owned a house and a candy store in the Red Hook section of Brooklyn, currently known as Carroll Gardens. The candy store was their main source of income, a meeting place for Italian immigrants, and my grandmother's first job. It was in that store where little Louisa first got her business sense and learned how to save a dollar.

My grandfather, Michael Caputo, was born in a little town in southern Italy called Mola di Bari, located on the coast of the Adriatic Sea. He was the second child out of six. His parents lived a simple life raising the children and growing vegetables.

My grandparents met each other in early 1925 and after dating a short while tied the knot on August 27, 1926. Their first apartment was on Coney Island Avenue in Brooklyn where they comfortably lived for a few years. During that time they had three kids, Grace, my father Pasquale and Salvatore. Salvatore unexpectedly died from pneumonia at the age of two. Months later my grandparents moved back to the old neighborhood and into their house on Second Place where they remained for nearly two decades.

Not long after the death of her youngest son, my grandmother lost her mother. That came as another shock and put more of a burden on her. My grandmother was overwhelmed and forced to divide her time, taking care of a sick father, her younger siblings and her own children. She even had relatives come to live with her and my grandfather. Aunt Grace said it was tough on everybody and very disruptive to her and my grandfather. Their marriage was beginning to disintegrate. My grandmother wanted to buy a house, but Grandpa didn't want to. The way she told me the story was "We started arguing over everything. Your grandfather was never ambitious and called me a 'showoff' because I wanted to buy a house. I could never understand him. He was a bricklayer with hands of gold. He had all the opportunity in the world to find us something affordable and good. But he was never interested! Poverty, The Depression, and your grandfather's stubbornness took its toll on our marriage." That story always made me sad. They separated on and off for years and for a short time my grandfather went back to Italy. When he returned, they reconciled and in the next couple of years had two more kids: Carol and Maria. A few years after they were born, my grandmother bought a house and her and grandpa called it quits for good.

Even though my grandmother was not a wealthy woman, she never looked to anyone for handouts. She worked hard as a seamstress to support her children and pay off the house. My grandmother basically survived on her salary and the little bit of rent she got from the tenants in the building. My grandfather was never any help, and she sometimes got ten to fifteen dollars a week from him which was nothing even in those days.

Meanwhile on the other side of Brooklyn, Angelina Nola (my mother's mother) was busy trying to raise her own kids. There were nine of them. One of them was Dolores (my mother). Dolores would marry Louise Caputo's son, Pasquale, in 1952. Later, Pasquale – who would change his name to Pat Cooper – would tell the story of their football wedding in his comedy act. This particular skit would appear on his first album "Our Hero," and it would end up being one of his most famous bits.

They moved into my grandmother's house where my sister and I were born. Life was good for my parents. They loved each other and tried for seven years to have kids. My mother took care of the house and stood by my father as he pursued his career. She went to every one of his gigs until I was born. I am the oldest and my sister was born two and a half years later. My father's career started to take off right around the time my sister was born and his success allowed him to meet a lot of people. One of those people was someone he had an affair with. After my mother caught on she threw him out for cheating. It was Valentines Day, 1960. I guess it was the seven-year itch and my father found someone to scratch it! I was two and a half years old and my sister was only two weeks old. My father left and we stayed in that upstairs apartment at my grandmother's house.

Life changed on a dime. My mother was in and out of family court. She was determined to make my father fulfill his obligations to my sister and I. He fought her every chance he got. I have to give her credit, he can be very intimidating, but her love for us and her drive to make sure we had what she didn't have growing up, was no match for him. My mom put us in Catholic school as she felt we would get a better education, the education she never had. My father fought her on that, too. My grandmother and my father were still in touch at this point. In one of their phone conversations my grandmother informed my father that my mother needed more money from him, as she couldn't pay the rent. My father's response was "throw them out!" My grandmother was furious with him. That was not an option for her and never was. We were her family, my mother included.

My grandmother was determined to keep the family together and wanted me and my sister to know and love her son. One day she told us she had a surprise for the both of us. She informed us that she was taking us to see my father perform at the Copa Cabaña in Manhattan. The Copa as it was known was where the biggest stars in show business did their shows. I was so excited at the thought of seeing my dad. She wanted me to see him and I think or should I say, I know she wanted to see him, too. She was very proud of him and happy that he had become successful. I often wonder if my father knew how much she loved him and how she encouraged my sister and I to love him, too. She held no grudges, my grandmother. He put her in the middle of his problems and she cleaned them up with the unconditional love that only a mother can have for her child. It was truly a thankless job.

My Grandmother wanted us to look great that night so we got all dressed up. I wore my best single-breasted suit with a matching tie and my sister wore a cute little dress. We felt so good that night we were going to see our father and more importantly we were going with grandma. She looked so elegant that evening and I could feel she was just as excited as we were.

When we arrived at the club we were escorted to the best table in the house. The place was dimly lit and we were seated up front in the center of the room. My father's new wife Patti and her nephew were seated at the table already. That was the first time I met her. It didn't even register with me that she was his new wife because I was so taken by how crowded the room was. Every table was filled with people eating and drinking. My dad came over to the table and welcomed us and informed the waiter to make sure we were comfortable and taken care of. I felt so special.

Connie Francis was the opening act for my father that evening. I knew who she was because my mother always played her records. She was amazing. Her voice sounded just like her records. Then after she had finished her last song there was a drum roll and then the emcee said "Ladies and gentleman, the Italian comedian Pat Cooper." The applause and cheers in the room where deafening. I just kept thinking to myself, is he going to bring me up on stage with him, is he going to mention me? I was so nervous. They played some Italian melody as my father entered the stage. He welcomed the adoring crowd. His routine mesmerized me. I was always a hyper kid but suddenly I was frozen in my seat. That was the first and last time in my life that I voluntarily sat still for over an hour. He was handsomely dressed in a tuxedo and the crowd loved him. He joked about my grandparents, and me and my sister, too. People were looking over at our table which made me feel a little uncomfortable. When he finished his act he came over to the table and joined us. He signaled to one of the photographers to take a picture of all of us. He put his arm around me as we posed for the picture. It was a special moment. I felt like he was back in my life. He wanted a picture of me so I thought everything was going to be fine from here on in. A few weeks later my grandmother presented me with that black and white picture and I immediately put it into my photo album for safe-keeping.

Every year at my school they had an event called the Communion Breakfast. It was held once a year and was just for fathers and their sons. My uncle Frankie always took me to these events but this particular year I asked my father to take me and he said yes. I couldn't believe it. He was famous now and everyone knew him as Pat Cooper. All the fathers at the breakfast recognized him and came over to the table to say hello. He introduced me to all of them and made me feel like I was the important one. He was finally the dad that I had hoped for. He wanted to be with me and he seemed proud that I was his son. It was a great day.

Life was going really well. My father started meeting me after school at the Purity restaurant, a small local diner located on 7th Ave, around the corner from my school. He would let me order anything on the menu and at times let me bring my friends, too. He would treat everybody and make us all laugh. He was so much fun to be around. I had two favorite dishes. My first choice was the hamburger special that came with fries and a soda. The second one was a bacon lettuce and tomato on toast with mayo, fries and a soda. I would alternate between my two favorites, but I always had to have a vanilla coke with my meal—the kind they made from the soda fountain. They would squirt sweet vanilla syrup into a glass filled with ice and coca cola. It was heaven. When we were alone, I purposely ate slowly just so I would have more time with him. I knew once I finished eating and the check came; it would be time for me to go home. Those lunches and the time spent with him meant the world to me.

Then after a while our lunch dates began to become fewer and fewer. The ones we did have began to consist of more silence than laughter. I would sit across from him and stare at him as he rolled a little ball of paper between his thumb and index finger wondering what was he thinking about. Was he bored with me already? Where was he? I knew he was sitting across from me, but it felt like he was a million miles away. Our lunches finally came to an end. I couldn't figure out what I had done to drive him away. Why didn't he want to spend time with me anymore?

My grandmother could feel that I was hurt and confused by his sudden disappearance. She told me that he was on the road traveling from city to city and that's why he couldn't meet me for lunch anymore. She reassured me that he loved me and that once things settled down for him he would be around again. I don't know if she really believed that or if she was just trying to make me feel better. What ever her reason was, it worked. My life returned back to normal with my father out of my life and my loving family—once again—there to fill in the void.

8

Chapter Two

- That's Amore -

In the absence of my father my childhood took place. I drove my mother and my grandmother crazy with all my nervous energy and practical jokes. My grandmother said I was a wreck and my mother said I had ants in my pants. My mother grew concerned and spoke to the doctor about my problem. He gave her a prescription for me to take. It was a clear liquid which looked like water and tasted very bitter. I had to take a tablespoon twice a day and that was supposed to do the trick. After a couple of days my mother saw something in my behavior that she didn't like. It relaxed me, but she thought a bit too much. On the third day she threw the bottle out. Instead of using a strong narcotic she decided to fix the problem herself by keeping me occupied and busy as much as she could.

My mother loved to take the bus and go shopping downtown to Fulton Street. Week after week she'd drag my sister and I in and out of all the department stores. We would get up early in the morning just to get there ten minutes before the stores opened. She made me believe if we weren't one of the first ones there, then they would have nothing left. I tried desperately to discourage her from taking me. Sometimes she would bribe me by telling me if I behaved that she would buy me a frankfurter and maybe a little toy. When that didn't work she knew she was going to have a day of hell. I could be a real pain in the ass. I would start whining to her about how bored I was as soon as we arrived at the stores. To occupy myself I invented a little game. I would pretend to be a monster and hide in the middle of the clothes rack. Then when a shopper walked by I would jump out of the rack and try to scare them. I had a lot of victims to choose from because the department stores were always mobbed. I thought it was funny, especially when I saw the look on their faces. Most of the time they were startled and other times they just gave me a dirty look. Some of them looked around to see if they could find my mother so they could tell her what I was doing. There was no way that I was going to let them find her so I'd run away and hide in the next rack to play my game all over again.

My grandmother had a different approach when I got out of line. One day my cousins came over and we went downstairs to play in the backyard. It was a small yard and consisted mostly of grass with a few tall trees and some flowers. She had a small statue back there and a clothesline. My grandmother liked to wash some of her clothes by hand and then hang them out to dry in the summer sun. I don't know why, but every time my cousins came over I liked to get wild and show off. We teamed up and decided to play a practical joke on grandma. Our plan was to dig a hole in the exact spot that grandma stood when she hung out the clothes. Then we would conceal it with some loose dirt and a large patch of grass that we pulled up from another section of the yard. When grandma came out to hang her clothes she would step into our booby trap, lose her balance, and fall in the hole. We both thought the idea was hysterical and couldn't wait to get started on my in-genious plan. We dug the hole and waited.

My cousins eventually left and later on that day I went down-stairs to feel my grandmother out. She seemed her normal self and didn't mention a thing. I snuck over to the window and took a little peek. Everything in the yard looked normal and I couldn't under-stand how she missed our trap. Then she asked me to do her a lit-tle favor—to look under the kitchen sink to make sure it wasn't leaking. I knelt down and stuck my head all the way in to see if there was any water under there. I was thinking to myself—she must be hearing things. What is she talking about? There's no leak in here. I heard her step away and go into the nearby closet where she kept all her pots and things. The next thing I knew I was being whacked on my butt with one of her brooms. She wasn't doing it hard enough to hurt me, but it scared the hell out of me. I jumped up and ran up-stairs to hide under the bed. "Don't think I didn't see what you and the other guy did in my yard. I could have broken my neck with your practical joke," she screamed as she chased me through the rooms. "What's wrong with you two? The next time I see the other guy he's going to get his head handed to him." I pleaded with her and kept on apologizing, over and over again, until she stopped shoving the broom under the bed. When she finally gave up and accepted my apology, I knew it was safe to come out.

They disciplined me in different ways. If I didn't do well in school my mother would threaten to throw one of my goldfish down the toilet bowl. I'd be sitting in class taking a test knowing that my poor fish's life depended on it. My grandmother on the other hand could sit there and give me the silent treatment for an hour just to get her point across. Then there would be other times she would fling the wooden spoon at me to show me who was boss. Whatever they did it worked and they always managed to keep me in line.

Like most kids I loved the summer! I would roller skate up and down the block and ride my bicycle all over the neighborhood. But without a doubt going to the beach was my favorite thing to do. We went to the same beach every year, Coney Island, and we always parked ourselves right in the middle of Bay 11. Between my mother and my grandmother we got to go all the time providing the weather permitted.

My grandmother loved the salt water and Coney Island was her second home. She would get up early, listen to the weather forecast, and sit in the backyard drinking her coffee. My sister and I would stare out the window waiting to get the signal from her to put on our bathing suits. Then she would go inside the house and get ready. She would pack her straw bag with squash and egg sandwiches, and meatball heroes, too. She filled her thermos with dark coffee and threw a few large beach towels into her straw bag. She liked taking her beach chairs along, but usually there was so much stuff, and never enough hands to carry them. We would run downstairs and she was ready to go. We hopped on the F train all the way to the West 8th Street station. It was fourteen stops to Coney Island from where we lived and I counted every one of them. My grandmother always took me to the first car so I could look out the window and pretend that I was driving the train. When we got off the train we entered onto a long walkway that led us to the boardwalk. I could smell the salt water and see the world famous Cyclone to my right. I watched in amazement as the roller coaster climbed the hill. The people sitting in the front car had their arms raised in the air as they approached the top. Then as they went over the top, screams of fear and excitement filled the air. Grandma looked at me and said, "Maybe I'll take you on a few rides later on if you behave yourself." I couldn't wait.

When we got to the boardwalk we were standing at Bay 11 right in front of The New York Aquarium. We went down a long wooden ramp that led us to the sand. Grandma would caution me to keep my shoes on until she opened the blanket because the sand was always very hot. All I could think about was jumping in the water and cooling off. She would put her large blanket down close to the shore because she wanted to keep an eye on us. Then I pulled off my clothes and ran towards the sea. It was freezing but over the years I learned to tolerate it. Then after awhile my lips would turn blue and my whole body would start shaking, and that's when I knew I had enough. I would run back to the blanket, wrap myself in a towel and dive into one of my grandmother's meatball heroes. She would sit on the blanket in her famous one-piece bathing suit, with a kerchief wrapped around her white bouffant hairdo. That was her trademark look and a good way of locating her on the crowded beach. Then she would take out a large jar of Noxzema and tell me to put some on her back.

After lunch, I would sit and wait for my Aunt Lily to arrive because she was the one who spent hours in the water with me. She would ride the waves all day and teach me how to swim. It didn't matter how cold the water was because when Aunt Lily was there I never wanted to get out. We would stay in the water until my grandmother signaled for us to come out. She would stand at the shore shaking her fist at us. But Aunt Lily and I would pretend not to see her. Finally, I would get out of the water and walk back to the blanket, cold and shivering. The first words out of my grandmother's mouth were: "Are yous blind? I've been calling the both of yous for an hour already!" I played stupid like I didn't know what she was talking about. She gave me one of her looks and handed me another sandwich. We stayed there late that day so I wasn't able to go on any of the rides. But I wasn't disappointed because I got to ride the waves all day with my aunt.

The next day my Aunt Grace and her kids came from New Jersey and went to the beach with us. I never got a chance to see them much because they lived so far away. They weren't crazy about the beach like we were because they hated sand. My grandmother knew this and had a plan. We would go to the beach only for a couple of hours, and then we would spend the rest of the day on the rides. This way she was certain we'd all be happy. I got up early that morning and looked out the window to do my usual weather check. I saw my cousins in the backyard and I ran downstairs. I got them all excited about the impending day as we packed up all our stuff. This time there were enough hands to carry grandma's beach chairs with us. I felt like a tour guide explaining to them all about Coney Island, the beach, and the rides. I didn't mind because this was the highlight of the summer for me.

I never went anywhere else in the summertime except to Casino pool with my mother's side of the family. It was the only salt water pool around and a long drive out to Freeport Long Island. We always had to depend on somebody in the family to drive us there. Besides, we were only able to go on the weekends because my uncles worked during the week. This large salt water pool had two diving boards and one of the highest slides in the world. I was always afraid of heights; it took me years to build up the courage to walk up those steps. Then once I got up there, I was afraid to come down. I managed to do it a few times with some coaching from my Uncle Frankie. That place had everything from shuffleboard courts, pinball machines, table tennis, to lockers and showers. They even had an area with swings for the adults and children. I enjoyed myself every time I went, but Coney Island was still my number one.

When we arrived at the beach we took a dip and then had our lunch. After lunch grandma always bought us a delicious cold 'fudgie wudgie' ice cream bar for dessert. There were always men carrying two or three brown shopping bags filled with knishes, soda and ice cream. They walked around all day in the heat proclaiming what goodies they had for sale.

Next, she took us over to the rocks and pointed out some crabs and black mussels. Some of my cousins didn't like fish so they were grossed out. I remember one time she took some of those black mussels home and cooked them for me. When I ate them, smothered in all that delicious spicy red sauce, I could still taste the sand. It didn't matter how many times she rinsed them, some of the sand would always remain in the shell. My grandmother always knew how to save a buck and was very creative, but I preferred when she bought them at the store.

After collecting some shells and taking another quick dip we were on our way over to Astroland. It was less than a five minute walk from Bay 11 and the entrance was located right off the boardwalk. This was the best part of the day because the place had every imaginable ride for the kids. There were roller coasters, spook houses, water log rides and even competitive games to play. When we entered the place my cousins' eyes lit up. From the expressions on their face I knew that they understood exactly what I told them earlier. They were in for a treat! I knew the place inside and out and grandma told me to pick five of my favorite rides. We walked by the water log and I told her that was the one I wanted us to go on first. She gave me the money and I ran to the ticket booth. Grandma stood outside the ride with all our things and her beach chairs, too. She watched as we boarded the log ride and instructed us to hold on. I let my cousins sit in the front because it was their first time, and I sat in the back to observe the whole thing. We were bouncing up and down on this rapidly moving water and headed towards the big hill. As we climbed the hill, I could see my grandmother waving to us. My cousins didn't even notice because they were frozen in their seats and too busy holding on as if their life depended on it. Then it went over the top and we started screaming our heads off. I got that familiar queasy feeling in my stomach as the log flew down the hill. When it hit the bottom the impact caused an enormous splash and whoever was sitting in the front took the brunt of it all. My cousin was soaked and immediately realized why I made him sit there. I guess that was sneaky of me, but I hated getting wet with all my clothes on.

Next we went on a couple of spinning rides. We slid in our seats from left to right with Motown music blasting in the background. The guy in the control booth kept asking us if we wanted more. Then he would speed up the ride even more if we responded. And of course we always did. We were having a ball. We came off that ride a little dizzy, so we decided to take a break and play some games. The games were fun because when you won they would give you a little prize. My grandmother always felt it was a scam and thought it was almost impossible to win. But if you did win, the prize was usually a stuffed animal or a single goldfish in a small bowl.

After a short losing streak playing different games, we were ready to go back on the rides. We saved the scariest ride of all, for last, which was the haunted house. I swear they had real people hanging out in there to try and scare you even more. It was pitch-black inside and as you rode through the rooms it felt like 'things' were touching you. Then when the chair whipped around one of the corners, a loud horn sounded off, and a tall boney skeleton appeared practically in your face. Turn the next corner, and it was the devil standing there with a pitchfork with long red horns sticking out the top of his head. We went on that ride twice and tried to persuade my grandmother to go on, too. She gave us one of her peculiar looks and said we were going back to the boardwalk to eat at Nathan's. She wanted to treat us to some of their delicious hot dogs and thick golden French fries. I wasn't hungry and still full from those sandwiches of hers. Instead, I was in the mood for something sweet and hoping that she would buy me some cotton candy. I wasn't sure if I could convince her, as she always tried discouraging me from eating that stuff. She told me it would make my teeth fall out. I watched my cousins devour their food while my grandmother went to get me some of my favorite pink sticky stuff. She wasn't saying no to anything that day, so I was in luck. She reluctantly handed it to me and said, "I don't know how you can eat this, it's all sugar! Don't tell your mother I bought you this crap." It was the end of the day; we were all content and spoiled silly. Now it was time to head back home.

As we were walking back to catch the train we were still talking about all the fun we had. Grandma was right behind us listening to every word we said. Then all of a sudden, just when we were about to enter the subway turnstile, she blurted out, "Where are my beach chairs?" I looked at my cousins, they looked at me, and we all looked at grandma. No one had an answer and we suddenly realized that we left them behind. It was too late to go back and look for them and it was obvious that we ruined her day. We were so caught up in all the fun and the excitement that we couldn't even remember the last time we saw those chairs. We apologized to her a hundred times. She wasn't angry with us, but she seemed disappointed. She spent a lot of money on us that day and I knew by now she was broke. I felt personally responsible for what happened because I was the leader of the pack. It was my job to keep an eye on everything. When we got home we were still bummed out about those chairs. She realized that and in a gentle tone she said, "If yous all had a good time today, then that's what really matters—forget about the chairs."

A couple weeks later I went back to the beach with my grandmother and let her down again. This time I ended up getting lost on her. It never happened before, not even with my mother. My mother tended to be a bit over-protective and my grandmother always gave me a little more freedom. I knew that and pushed my luck that day. I started walking along the shore and decided to investigate the other bays. They were no different from Bay 11 but I had the urge to do some exploring anyway. I figured I could slip away from my grandmother and return before she even noticed I was gone. I lost track of time and realized that I was lost. I didn't think that could happen because I had two great landmarks to find my way back to the blanket—the Cyclone roller coaster and the flag-like kerchief wrapped around my grandmother's head. Those were two constants and I thought all I had to do was walk in their direction. But something was terribly wrong, because from where I was standing I couldn't see either one.

I began to panic and started to cry. I don't remember if I was crying because I got lost or what my grandmother was going to do to me when she found me. Some lady saw me crying and helped me find a cop. They asked me some questions and I told them my grandmother's blanket was somewhere by the shore straight down from the New York Aquarium.

Within a half an hour they located my grandmother. I was so happy to see her, but again, thought she was going to kill me. It turned out she was more worried than I was. She felt bad and took me back to the blanket where she was very comforting. She knew I learned my lesson and that it would make no sense to lecture me and make me feel worse. After that ordeal I never wondered off again nor had the desire to do anymore exploring at the beach.

The more I think about Coney Island the more I realize it was a blessing. It was the poor man's vacation, as my grandmother would always say, and I never felt that I needed to be anywhere else. My grandmother gave me a profound appreciation for that beach and I am forever grateful to her and my mother for the amount of time that we spent there. I grew up on Bay 11 and have many fond memories of that place, thanks to them. I often wondered had my mother and father stayed together if I still would have gone to the beach as much. Maybe my sister and I would have gone to camp or went on a real vacation, like Disneyland. I would sometimes find myself daydreaming about what it would be like to go on a real vacation. I wished that one day my father would call and surprise me with an exciting trip. My birthday was in July so I thought maybe he would call then and give me a birthday vacation. But deep down inside I knew that if my father never even sent me a birthday card, then chances were he wasn't going to give me any gifts either. I remained hopeful and dreamed about it anyway. I think my grandmother knew that and had a plan.

That summer my grandmother surprised me with a trip to a mountain resort as an early birthday present. She booked a trip to a quiet resort located way up in the Pocono Mountains. Nearby they had a special kind of zoo where I could feed and pet the animals. Then at nighttime they had all kinds of entertainment including live music, dancing, shows, and contests. Grandma never traveled alone so we were joined by her sisters Mary, Rose, and Lily. Aunt Mary had a car, and whenever that little group came along, you could be sure it was going to be fun and adventurous.

After our long ride we had to check in to this cabin-like motel. It was a peaceful rural setting that was very crowded with families checking in and out. One by one we got our keys and had to walk up a hill to get to our rooms. I was busy looking around and I was happy to see that there were plenty of kids my age there. I knew by the time we left I would make a couple of new friends.

When we got to our rooms I noticed they all looked the same. They had two large beds, a small bathroom, a few lamps and a little desk. There was one large piece of furniture in the middle of the room that had deep draws for all our things. Everything looked old and used, but nevertheless, the place still had a cozy little feel to it. The first thing grandma did was unpack everything and then we went to get something to eat. We entered a large dining area that displayed a spectacular buffet. I liked the way they had it set up because we could help ourselves to a variety of food and deserts, even two or three times if we wanted.

Once we were done eating my grandmother took me over to the game room. I got to spend at least an hour in there playing on my favorite pinball machines. Then we walked all around to familiarize ourselves with the place. My grandmother wanted to find out what was on the agenda for the rest of the week so she could plan our days accordingly. After she found out everything she needed to know, she took me by the pool for the rest of the day.

The next morning at breakfast grandma gave me all the details. First we were going into town for a scenic ride on a ski lift.

Then we would go to the zoo like she promised. After dinner we would walk around the grounds for awhile, and then off to see a show at the nightclub.

Even though it was summer my grandmother found a place that gave rides on a ski lift for the fun of it. We both sat in a small chair with only a single metal bar across our stomachs holding us in. I was never crazy about heights, but never said anything to anyone. And I knew my grandmother wouldn't take no for an answer, anyway. The higher it climbed the more frightened I became and it didn't help that the wind was picking up speed. It made the carriage shake and I could hear the rusty wheels on the cable beginning to squeak. I looked up and realized we were at the mercy of a single metal rope pulling us along only a few feet above the tall trees. She told me to enjoy the ride and not to look down if it made me sick. I sat back and closed my eyes a few times but that didn't help, it made me dizzier. I couldn't understand how my grandmother got enjoyment out of staring at the top of so many trees. Then she looked at me and told me to smile because they would be taking a picture of us as we made our way back down.

Going to the zoo was the best part of the day and I got to go on another ride. It wasn't a high one this time, but a long one on the back of a real donkey. We also went to an area where we could pet and feed some of the small animals. They sold us some food at the entrance and told us not to put any of it in our pockets or into any other packages that we were carrying. My aunt Lily and I were walking around and feeding the whole place. She put the bulk of the food into her pocket book. Aunt Lily knew she wasn't supposed to do that. While we were busy feeding half the place, one of the animals came from behind and aggressively put his face into her bag. With a startled look on her face my aunt pulled her pocket book from the animal's mouth. In a matter of minutes all the animals in the place surrounded us. We just threw the food at them and ran. We jumped back into the car and laughed about it all the way back to the dinner table.

19

After dinner we went back to the room to get ready for this costume contest that I heard them talking about all day. I was under the impression that they had already bought me something to wear when we were in town and they were going to surprise me. But the rules were that the costume had to be an original one and not something that you purchased. One thing I can say; it was a surprise and it definitely was an original. They had planned to dress me up as a girl using an item or two from each of their wardrobes to create my costume.

At first I thought they were kidding with me. But when I saw them going through all the draws, that's when I knew they were serious. I told them I didn't want to be a girl and would rather be one of my favorite super heroes. But they continued fussing with their clothes and trying to convince me. I told my grandmother that I would be very embarrassed if somebody recognized me and told my friends. She knew I worried about everything and reassured me that there wasn't anybody up in the Poconos that knew us.

First they tried on Aunt Rosie's wig and that was too big so they gave me Aunt Lily's. It was a brown-teased wig that hugged my face. It was the same style as my grandmother's hair except they wanted me to be a brunette. It was a perfect fit to my surprise, but it was itchy and uncomfortably warm under that thing. Then Aunt Rosie handed me her blouse. That became my dress that barely went down to the top of my knees. It was a horizontally striped dress that had every color of the rainbow on it. They took a thin black rope and tied it around my waist to act as a belt. Then they opened a new package of beige panty hose and my toe nail ripped through one of them while trying to put them on. They looked terrible because they made my legs look skinnier than they already were. Now my legs were a different color and looked so feminine and petite.

Fifteen minutes had past and they were still taking out more stuff. Aunt Rosie took out these long white gloves that went practically up to my elbows. I started thinking about what would happen when I have to use the bathroom and I can't get all this stuff off in time? And when I get to the club which bathroom should I use the urinal in the men's room or the toilet seat in the women's? Just thinking about all this made me nervous.

Last but not least they took out the white patent leather shoes with the medium heels. They were a little big for me so they filled in the spaces with some toilet paper. My bra was already filled with a whole roll of toilet paper to give me a C-cup. I thought they were finished but they had a few more accessories in mind. My grandmother handed me her long white pearl necklace and a matching pair of clip-on earrings. Those gold clips were killing me and made my earlobes all red. Aunt Lily completed my look by decorating me with her costume jewelry and a little black beaded pocket-book.

I tried to pull away and look at myself in the mirror but they came at me with their entire make up collection. They were smearing liquid foundation all over my face and drawing lines on my hairless eyebrows. It was too late to change my mind or make a run for it, especially with those heels on. They told me to stop fidgeting as they proceeded to apply some eye mascara and a lot of red lipstick. My grandmother wanted me to have a beauty mark that looked just like hers. So she took a long black pencil and drew one on the left side of my face that looked like it was the size of a dime.

I was anxious to see the finished product. I ran over to the full length mirror and almost broke my neck. My feet were still slipping and sliding even with all that toilet paper they put in there. I looked in the mirror and realized that they had disguised me pretty well. No one could possibly recognize me like this, and that was a very comforting thought. They managed to make me look like a younger version of the three of them. Who else could I possibly look like? I was related to them and wearing half their wardrobe. I kept staring at myself and wondering how I was going to face the people at the club. My grandmother told me to get my purse and we went on our way.

When I got to the club I immediately recognized all of the contestants. They were the same kids that I had played with in the game room. They all had normal looking costumes on and I knew every one of them. My grandmother and her sisters took the seats right in the front and immediately sent me up to the stage. My knees felt weak but I stood there smiling with the rest of them as the emcee warmed up the audience. I could see the other kids looking at me and trying to figure out who I was. The emcee went over to each kid and asked them their name. Then he discussed their costume and waited for the audience to applaud. The winner would be determined by the intensity of the last round of applause.

Little by little I could see that he was making his way over to me. It was obvious that I was going to be the last one. Finally, turning to me and smiling, his opening line was, "Well, what do we have here...and look at those terrific legs?"

Before I could even answer him the audience was hysterical. I felt stupid and looked like an alien, but still managed to keep a smile on my face. He saw how self-conscious I was and proceeded to ask me my name. I thought he meant a stage name, so I told him my name was Louise. I was so nervous and my grandmother's name was the first name that popped into my head. The audience lost it. Even the kids in the contest were laughing at me.
"No tell us your real name not an alias," he said.
"Oh!" I replied. "My name is Michael Caputo."

He quickly faced the audience and on the loud microphone he announced, "Ladies and Gentlemen, we have a celebrity on our stage. Here you have standing before you is the son of the famous Italian comedian, Pat Cooper." I almost died! Who told him? One thing for sure, it wasn't my grandmother. She never went around telling anybody about that. It definitely had to be one of my aunts. I could have killed them! Now everybody knew who I was. He asked for another round of applause and I was obviously the winner.

22

I looked at the table and saw my grandmother smiling. Somehow, for better or worse, they managed to pull this off. We went back to the room and it took forever to wash off all that makeup. They were very happy that I won and you could tell that they had more fun than I did. It was one of those things that you never forget, a first vacation and my last time in drag.

The next night we went back to the club to see another show and listen to the band. I didn't see any kids in the place, but the same emcee was there talking and joking with the audience. When we walked in he recognized us and called me back up to the stage. He told everybody that I won a contest the previous night, and that I was Pat Cooper's son. He made me take a bow and handed me one of the band's drumsticks. The band began to play some music and he demonstrated how I was supposed to conduct them. I was all dressed up standing center stage and leading all of the musicians. He let me do that for about twenty minutes and I felt like a million bucks.

When we got home my grandmother gave me three photographs as souvenirs: the first one was the both of us on the ski lift ride, the second was me in drag, and the third was me conducting the band. I never understood how my grandmother got so many pictures; she never owned a camera. I still have all three photographs saved in my photo album with the other pictures my grandmother gave to me. I didn't get a card or even a phone call from my father on my birthday. But I did get a few memorable photographs from grandma as a reminder of my first real summer vacation.

Chapter Three

- Home -

The new semester brought a lot of unwelcome changes. I began to get a lot of headaches in school and had trouble seeing the blackboard. The teachers contacted my mother and suggested she take me to have my eyes checked. Her suspicions turned out to be correct and I ended up needing glasses. I was never crazy about wearing them and thought they made me look like a geek. I only had to wear them in class and when I did my reading homework.

Not long after getting my glasses, I went down to the corner store and bought some candy. I remember it being a small package of m & m's with peanuts. I put one of them in my mouth, bit down and felt a sharp pain all the way up to my head. My mother thought I had chipped my tooth and brought me to the dentist. It turned out that I had a cavity. I felt like I was in that chair for hours as the dentist filled my back tooth with all that silver. When in actuality the whole experience was more like twenty-minutes. I was so relieved when I finally got out of that office of pain, and thought I would never have to return. Oh how wrong I was!

Not long after my m & m nightmare, the dentist informed my mother that I needed braces. I thought my life was over. I now would be the kid in school with braces and glasses. My mother contacted my father and told him the news. She dreaded asking him for anything because he always gave her and the doctors a hard time. On my next visit to the dentist office I overheard the dentist telling my mother that my father had complained about having to pay for my braces. My father knew he was responsible for all our doctor bills. I don't know if it was him or his new wife Patti that would intentionally delay the payment. It was not only embarrassing, but meant another trip down to family court.

My father made my nightmare of getting braces even worse. I already had to wear glasses and now I had to wear braces. I knew I was going to get teased at school and my father never even called me to say be strong son, or give me a pep talk. All he cared about was that it was going to cost him money.

I had to wear a pink bulky retainer and every month we had to go to the orthodontist office and check out my progress. To make matters worse, whenever I read out loud in class it would sound like I had a lisp. Some of the kids would laugh at me and I became very self-conscious. When it came time to that part of the day, I'd hide behind the kid in front of me so the teacher couldn't see me. After a while that didn't work anymore, so I just pulled the retainer out of my mouth whenever I was called upon to read.

My mother was determined to make sure that I had a healthy self-esteem so she entered my sister and I in a talent contest at our school. My sister did a little dance that my mother taught her and I sang a popular tune, acappella. She wore a cute puffy dress and I wore my suit. I went out first and was all ready until I stepped out on the stage. Then all of a sudden I froze. I opened my mouth, took a deep breath, and rushed through the whole song. I took a quick bow and ran off the stage knowing that I forgot some of the words. The audience applauded anyway. When my sister came out she stole the show with her little dance and the outfit that my mother dressed her in. It was our first try at show business and my first bout with stage fright. Our debut made my mother proud.

That year, every time I turned around, I was either at the dentist office or seeing a doctor for something. I always carried on and gave my mother a hard time whenever the doctor had to come to the house. In those days doctors made house calls when their patients were sick. As soon as I heard his footsteps coming up the stairs I would run into the bathroom and lock myself in. My mother and the doctor would be on the other side of the door pleading with me to open it and come out. I was so tense and afraid that I'd be leaning up against the door with all my strength so they couldn't push it in. I stood in the bathroom with a stubborn refusal to come out until the doctor left. All I could think about was that big needle he wanted to stick me with.

My mother called the doctor only when it was absolutely necessary. She dreaded all that rigmarole that I put her through. She did have another option that I preferred and there were no needles involved. My mother knew there was always the advice of my grandmother who was located only two floors below. Grandma didn't believe in doctors and had a few remedies of her own that she believed could cure us. Whenever I got a chest cold that wouldn't go away my grandmother knew how to get rid of it once and for all. She went to the store and bought some mustard powder and some thin white cloth. She cut the cloth into eight inch square pieces. She put the powder in a dish and poured in some warm water. Then she mixed it all together to form a thick moist paste. She took her spatula and spread the mustard paste on a piece of thin cloth. Then she covered it with another piece of cloth making it look like a large sandwich. Then she placed them in the oven to heat them up. When she took them out you could see that the cloth absorbed most of the water. She placed one of them on my chest. It smelled weird and it was so hot my chest turned all red. She left it on for a while and took out the next one. When we were done she put some Vicks Vapor Rub on my warm chest and told me to sleep with a white undershirt on. I could feel it working immediately. The next day when I woke up, my breathing felt better and my wheezing was gone.

She also used Vicks Vapor Rub when I had a cold or trouble breathing out of my nose. She would place the whole jar into a steaming pot of water. Then she'd have me put a towel over my head with my face and nose directly over the steaming pot. She told me to inhale a few times until I could feel my sinuses open. In no time I felt like I could breath freely again.

Whether it was the common cold or a twenty-four hour virus, my grandmother would always recommend her favorite cure: a "physic." That's what they called an "enema" back in her day. She swore by that thing and felt we should all give ourselves one on a

Michael Caputo

regular basis in order to keep our bodies healthy. She believed it was the only way to really clean your system and eliminate the toxins from your body. That was her prescription and the first thing she told everybody to do when they got sick. We used to laugh and tease her about it all the time. I don't know if it was those remedies, the love behind them, or a combination of both that made us feel better. One thing for sure; they always worked!

The winter was in full swing and I couldn't wait for the first snowfall. There was something about watching the snow falling from my apartment window that had a calming effect on me. When I was a kid it meant sleigh riding, snowball fights and who could build the biggest snowman. If I was lucky it meant a few days off from school, too.

Well the day came and we had a blizzard. Park Slope looked so majestic covered in a thick blanket of snow and surrounded by tall luminescent trees blooming with icicles. I only had one thing on my mind when I saw it snow like that, but I had to patiently wait for my grandmother to get home from work to make it a reality. I always knew when she got home because I could hear her unlock the middle door. That door led to a back staircase on the second floor inside the building. She always left it opened for me and my sister. She knew once she unlocked it that it would only be a matter of time before I came running downstairs to greet her. If I didn't hear her unlock the door then I knew she was home by the smell of her cooking coming up through the vents. I immediately got my coat and ran downstairs to her house as fast as I could. She took one look at me and knew what I wanted. She told me to fetch the sled in the cellar and then go back upstairs to get my sister. Before I knew it we were all outside and headed up the block. There was no traffic that night because of the storm. Grandma placed the sled in the middle of the street and my sister and I sat in position. We were all ready and bundled up for the occasion in the coats that she made for us. They were warm bulky coats with oversized hoods. "Hold on," she said, as she grabbed the rope attached to the front of the sled. We started moving slowly then grandma picked up some speed. We were screaming our heads off and I was thinking I could do this all night. We didn't feel the cold and lost all track of time. "Okay, once more," she said. Grandma's cheeks and nose were a rosy red and it looked like she was slowing down. She worked all day making coats, shoveled the sidewalk, cooked dinner, and now she was out in the snow playing with us. We weren't even thinking about what her day was like. We were kids and oblivious to everything else except the fun we were having. "Okay, this is the last one!" she shouted. I didn't believe her because she had been saying that for the last fifteen minutes. I knew, even if she was serious, that she would somehow find the energy to pull us up and down the block a few more times. Then she hurried us in for something warm to eat. I don't know where all that stamina came from; maybe from all the macaroni she ate. I mean, she was almost sixty years old and gave us an awesome time.

It never did snow again that year, at least not in blizzard amounts. But there was something bigger than a snowfall to look forward to. It was my favorite time of the year because the holidays were just around the corner.

My grandmother made Christmas a major event at her house. As I mentioned earlier, my father learned the art of entertaining from my grandmother and Christmas was her biggest show of the year.

A day before Christmas Eve she began the pre-production work for her big Christmas spectacular. She ran everything like a finely oiled machine. First thing on her to-do list was a trip to the Fulton Fish Market in lower Manhattan. That's where she would purchase all the fish in large quantities at wholesale prices. Well, this particular year I had been promoted to production assistant and was lucky enough to go with her on her yearly early morning pilgrimage. We got up at 4 o'clock in the morning, had a light breakfast, and hurried outside to meet Aunt Carol who was already waiting in her car with Aunt Marie. My aunt Carol is an amazing artist and she brought along a small film crew to document grandma's ritual. It was a great idea because we would have grandma's whole Christmas spectacular on tape forever.

When we arrived at the market I could see the early sunrise. The first thing I noticed was how beautiful the Brooklyn Bridge looked silhouetted against the sky. It was still dark outside and there were trucks everywhere. My grandmother stepped out of the car and led the way through a makeshift doorway into what seemed like one very large room. There were large silver scales that lined the metal tables which were filled with crushed ice and fresh fish. My grandmother walked around there like she owned the place. Determined and self-confident she was ready to begin the bargaining. "Who's got the clams this year? How much do you get for a bushel? What do you get for a pound of shrimp? I need ten pounds!" Over and over again she played this game. The men got a kick out of her and one of them even pretended that he was going to pick her up and place her in the scale. "Does anybody have snails for my grandson, she screamed?" In about forty-five minutes she found everything she was looking for, except the snails. She knew I liked them and promised to get them for me back in the neighborhood. She paid all the men in cash and had them pack up the car. We were on our way home, mission accomplished.

I sat in the car and realized that the overwhelming fish smell was coming home with us. There were two bushels of live fish in the back seat with me. I tried to take a nap but kept one eye opened just in case one of those lobsters or crabs got loose. I wonder if they knew they would be on our dinner table tomorrow night. When we got home my grandmother put the fish in the front vestibule. It was cold enough to keep them fresh till the next day. I told all the kids on the block about my grandmother's temporary pets in the wooden boxes. They didn't believe me so she took out a few lobsters and placed them down in her front yard. The kids all started screaming, laughing, and scattering about. My grandmother pointed out that the lobsters couldn't bite anyone. She went on to explain; as long as they had the tape holding their claws shut, they were harmless. Those kids were not convinced, but still enjoyed my grandmother's little show.

The sight of the lobsters was just the beginning of all the work that lied ahead. The fish had to be cleaned and cooked by 6 pm the next day. My grandmother had a passion for cooking and it was a way of keeping the family together. Through the years she gave us enough nourishment that filled our stomachs and our hearts. The familiar smells and flavors gave us a sense of home and tradition that united us like the ingredients in her cooking. My earliest image of my grandmother is seeing her in the kitchen with her apron tied around her waist. Wearing her soiled yellow mittens and leaning over the sink pouring hot water from a large pot filled with boiled macaroni. This is a common flashback of my grandmother that we all share. It is one of my favorite mental pictures of her and always puts a smile on my face.

My grandmother always had a few helping hands and this year it was my turn to join the crew. I didn't know what I was getting myself into and it didn't turn out to be as much fun as the trip to the fish market. Grandma orchestrated the cleaning process and decided who was doing what. She placed ten pounds of shrimp in front of me and told me to watch her closely. In twenty minutes I was on my own. She went to the kitchen to soak all the clams, that way they would be a lot easier for Aunt Carol to open. She made all the stuffing for the clams and a large pot of marinara sauce. I finished the shrimp and she proceeded to bread them. I was starving so she fried a few to hold me over till suppertime. Aunt Carol was finished opening the clams and I caught her eating a few. I only liked them baked so I was out of luck till later on. Everyone was busy doing something and we were in the final stages of the cooking. Then grandma commanded us to throw out all the garbage and get the table ready. I brought the aluminum table up from the cellar to accommodate the hungry guests. It was 6 o'clock exactly when the doorbell rang. SHOW TIME! That was the sound I'd been waiting for all day.

The family started pouring in and within thirty minutes the place was packed. Everyone was in a festive mood. There were kisses exchanged and joyful shouts of Merry Christmas. Grandma wasted no time and supplied both tables with trays of antipasto,

31

Italian bread and some wine. In the kitchen she poured the bubbling red calamari sauce over a large bowl of spaghetti. She carried it to the center of the table, looked at us with her familiar smile and said, "Dig in!" We were all ready. I tried not to eat so much spaghetti because I wanted to save room for the lobsters and my baked clams. I knew I could easily finish off about a dozen clams and a lobster or two. Just when I thought I had no more room my grandmother brought out a bowl of snails just for me. I thought she forgot. She placed them in my plate and said, "I found these for you this morning." Then she handed me a safety pin and told me to enjoy.

After dessert we couldn't move. We remained at the table to digest our food and continue our conversations. Grandma used this time to relax and tell us a few of her own funny stories. There is no question that this was the highlight of the year for her. Not only because it was Christmas Eve, but also because she brought the family together once again.

Sooner or later even our close friends spent a holiday or two at my grandmother's house. Her open door policy was a reflection of the kind-natured person that she was. Everybody attended those fabulous dinners at one time or another, except my father. He never participated in any of the family celebrations from the time he and my mother got separated. He never sent any gifts to the house or even called to wish us a happy holiday. I remember sitting at the table wondering if he was thinking of us. Who was he with? Was he doing a show that night? If he wasn't performing then why didn't he want to celebrate the holidays with all of us? Fortunately, my sister and I were blessed with a loving family that filled in the gap.

On Christmas Eve my sister and I were always in bed before midnight. Mom told us, "The faster you fall asleep, the faster Santa Claus will come." I was so excited and kept thinking about all the presents he was going to leave at our house. I concentrated very hard and finally dozed off. I knew if I didn't fall asleep right away, Santa wouldn't come, and I would ruin the most important day of the year for my sister and I.

Mom worked diligently for hours wrapping our presents and setting up the living room. Then at 7 o'clock in the morning she'd wake us up and tell us that Santa just left. We both raced into the living room to be greeted by a spectacular display of colorful gifts. My mother's strategy was always one big gift surrounded by a bunch of small ones. The big gifts were all set up and placed in the middle of the room to catch our eyes first. The smaller ones were always meticulously wrapped and placed under the Christmas tree signed from Santa.

I don't know how my mother was able to shower us with a complete gamut of awesome gifts. I had fish tanks, Lionel trains and a couple of racing car sets. My sister got the latest dolls and their matching wardrobes. She also got baby carriages, make-believe ovens and a large dollhouse. We both would sit around the tree with our favorite toy and play pretend. I could race those miniature cars around the figure-eight track all day. There were so many gifts that it looked like Santa only came to our house. All we wanted to do was just stay home and play with our toys. But we knew the routine.

Christmas Day we would spend with my mother's side of the family. It was a large family and I got a chance to see my cousins and play with some of their toys, too. All my aunts were great cooks and their specialty for Christmas Day was lasagna. It always turned out to be a great day and lots of fun. After dessert it was time to leave and one of my uncles would always drive us home. We usually ended up falling asleep in the back seat of the car. Our bellies were full and so was the car with more shopping bags filled with gifts from my aunts and uncles. We knew Christmas was over, but we still had a few more days to play with our toys before we returned back to school.

The next biggest religious holiday in the Catholic religion was Easter. In my house it meant the arrival of spring, coloring eggs and large chocolate bunnies. It also meant a week off from school. My mother and grandmother never made a big deal of it like they did for Christmas. My mother taught us how to color eggs and surprised us in the morning with some chocolate left by the Easter bunny. My grandmother hid a few candy baskets around the house and told us whatever we found we could keep. Grandma enjoyed the spring and liked to relax in the yard with her coffee. Often she would put me to work by having me weed the lawn and turn the soil. Easter week was also the time of the year that my grandmother was very busy doing her yearly baking.

During my week off I took the opportunity to watch her bake. I wanted to see how she turned a pile of dough into fabulous little cookies and cakes. A lot of work went into all that, but nevertheless, I wanted to watch and maybe participate.

She took out a big rolling pin and put the white round table in the center of the kitchen. Then she scattered some flour on top of it. Using a small knife she proceeded to cut the dough. She grabbed a small chunk from this yellowish mass and with the rolling pin stretched it out as wide as the table. Over and over again she pushed her weight into it until it was thin and perfect. Then she cut the dough into thin strips and showed me how to shape them into bows and ribbons. She told me and Aunt Lily to put the pies in the oven to bake. We both were looking for a match to light it while my grandmother went outside to throw the garbage. We couldn't find one so we lit a long piece of newspaper on the stove and stuck it by the hole in the center of the oven. We turned the switch on to 350 degrees and nothing happened. By the time my grandmother came back in the house the kitchen was filled with smoke. She walked in and saw my miniature torch. She let out a scream then shouted, "What the hell are yous trying to do, burn my house down?" "Don't yous know whenever you turn on the oven there is always a slight delay? You have to wait a few seconds, and then it starts by itself." We didn't know that and thought we had to help it along like we used to do with her old oven. I kept thinking about what could have happened if she didn't come back in the house and rescue us. We were the main topic of conversation that holiday and every Easter after that my grandmother reminded me of our little mishap just to make sure I never touched her oven again.

It was around this time that my mother started to go out on Friday nights. It was her way of taking a break from her weekly routine. She and her girlfriend would go out dancing. I'd be watching my favorite cartoon, the Flintstones, while she was getting ready. She always put on her most beautiful dress and her matching high-heeled shoes. Then right before she left, she'd do her make up, spray on some sweet smelling perfume, and then give me and my sister a great big kiss. Going out one night a week kept my mother sane and gave her an opportunity to meet someone. She was still a young woman and was separated from my father for a few years already. My sister and I never made a fuss and were usually left with my grandmother or a babysitter.

One of those Friday nights my mother met someone. She met a nice man named Walter. She dated him for months before she brought him into our lives. My mother was very protective of us and never allowed any strange men in our house. So when she introduced us to her new friend, I knew it was serious. He would meet us at school and take us out to lunch in his Volkswagen Beetle. At nighttime he took us on long rides out to the airport. Then he'd park the car and open the roof so my sister and I could watch the airplanes take off and land. Those are my earliest memories of my stepfather.

A year later, unknowingly to me, my mother and Walter were ready to take a big step. She knew Walter was the person she could trust and that he had only the best intentions for her and the kids. For me, it was all so sudden and unexpected when my mother told me that we were moving.

I didn't know what to do. My grandmother's house was all I ever knew. It was in her house that my mother taught me how to pray and grandma taught me what to pray for. My mother educated me and grandma taught me my most valuable lessons. My mother protected me from the cold and grandma made the coats to keep me warm. My mother gave me life and grandma showed me how to make the best of it. All my memories were in that house. I felt safe and secure there. That day, in the blink of an eye, my whole world changed!

Chapter Four
- Little Boy Blue -

We moved in with Walter and his mother into a small one-bedroom apartment on Avenue P and Dahill Road. The first thing I noticed about the place was that it wasn't big enough for all of us to live there. From day one, I felt crowded and uncomfortable. It was dark and dreary looking, and simply furnished; two beds in the bedroom, and a convertible couch in the living room. It was located on a busy two-way street that had more apartment buildings than private homes. There were no stoops to sit down on and no place to play. I hated the place!

My mother tried her best to excite us about our new home and new family. She did everything in her power to make all the adjustments more comfortable. She even kept us in our old school. But being ten years old, the only thing I could think about was the old neighborhood, and all the fun I used to have there. It was such a hassle going to school by train every morning but I was grateful that I was in my old neighborhood 5 days a week. My mother was never a big fan of the trains, so that didn't last very long. It was too much for all of us and that's when we started taking a cab to school.

It was a scenic ride and the cab driver became our friend. His name was Joe, and he would pick us up every morning at exactly the same time. When we reached our destination we'd kiss mom goodbye, and then for the rest of the day she waited for us in the neighborhood. She accompanied us for months and then we started going alone. It was the same routine for over a year.

Joe the cab driver was always reliable and made our thirty-minute ride very entertaining. I remember that he liked his job, his cigarettes and his gambling. One day he had a hunch and asked me to give him a "three number." I had no idea what he meant. He explained that he wanted me to pick a random number between 100 and 999. We were riding along and the first number I saw was an address on a house. It read 427. I felt it was a good number and I quickly shouted it out. He didn't say anything more, and never told me the reason why he wanted it. The next morning when he came by to pick us up he was all smiles. He told my mother that he won on the lucky number that I gave him. He handed me a one hundred dollar bill and told us he was going to Puerto Rico with his wife. It all seemed so easy and after that I tried giving him a winning number everyday.

Soon it would be summer and that presented another challenge. It was time to go outside and see if I could make some friends. First, I tried hanging out in front of the building but that didn't work. There were gossipy old ladies sitting out there and they always complained to the landlord if anyone made noise. So I roamed around the neighborhood just to get away from them. I knew it was only a matter of time before I ran into somebody my own age.

One summer day I heard the sound of kids playing outside by our kitchen window. I looked across the courtyard and I could see that the house next door had a four-foot round swimming pool. There were a couple of kids jumping off the ladder and doing cannonballs in the water. I made up my mind at that moment that I was going to do everything in my power to befriend them.

My first friend was a Jewish boy that lived down the hall from me. He was a nice kid who had over protective religious parents. His mother never let him do anything or go anywhere. One day we were playing in his house and I started to tell him all about Christmas and Santa Claus. When his mother heard that she quickly intervened. She appeared annoyed and told me that he doesn't believe in Santa Claus. She went on to say that they weren't Catholic and Santa Claus doesn't exist. I was shocked when she told me that and I felt sorry for my friend. I was eleven years old and had my doubts about Santa, but I didn't need her to break it to me that way. After that day I never felt comfortable enough to go back in their house and I remained somewhat distant from my friend.

I set out to find someone else to play with and that's when I remembered the kid next door who had the pool. He always played in the front yard with his dog and I wanted to join him. One day when I passed by his house I started a conversation with him and started to pet his dog. In no time I was in the yard playing with them and we became friends. I used to go there often and I thought, sooner or later, he would invite me in his pool. But in the two summers that we lived there, I only went in once. His parents never even invited me in the house. Back in my old neighborhood we all played and ate in each other's homes like we were family. It was a bumpy start for the first summer living there, but I got what I wanted, and finally made some new friends. I learned one of my first lessons in life: Everybody isn't going to be as kind and friendly like our family was.

Once fall arrived we were back to our regular routine. It wasn't my favorite time of the year because it meant back to school. It would be getting dark earlier and we were always bombarded with so much homework. There was no time to go out and play or watch any television. Then before we knew it Walter was home and it was time for dinner.

One night while we were eating I found out that Walter's mother was moving out. She was going to live with her daughter, and Walter's son, Michael, would soon be moving in with us. I was excited about that because I thought I was going to have another friend that I could play with. I soon realized that he was sixteen years old and a little bit too old for me. We got along very well, despite our age difference, and he taught me how to play the drums. We had a big drum set in the corner of the living room, and I was impressed whenever he played. It was fun while it lasted and eventually the landlord told us we had to cut out the noise.

Everything always went wrong at that place. They even got me a dog because they knew how much I loved animals. I had all kinds of pets like: parakeets, canaries, fish, and turtles. My mother didn't want the dog because there was no room, and it required a lot more work than a bird or a fish. She was totally against the idea but somehow Walter convinced her.

My step-brother named him Shadow and my mother always kept him tied up in the kitchen. She was strict and didn't want him roaming the house. His was a medium size dog, a black and white mutt with a lot of energy. He didn't like being restricted and every time we went out he would tear up the kitchen carpet. Over and over again, Walter repaired it. After the third time my mother told us we had to get rid of him. My sister and I begged them to give Shadow another chance. Walter decided to buy some extra-strength glue that was sure to hold the carpet down. It looked like it was working for a while because for a couple of weeks it was left untouched. Then one day we came home to a horror scene in the kitchen. The dog had ripped up the carpet again and vomited all over the floor. He was very sick and the whole apartment stunk. Shadow had ingested too much glue and ruined the carpet for the last time. The next day Walter took the dog someplace and that was the end of Shadow. My sister and I were devastated!

I hated living on Dahill Road! I never felt like we belonged there and I can't think of anything about that place that I even liked. It was the first major change in my life and I had a hard time adjusting to it. I missed my grandmother, my friends, and the comforts of living in a real home.

In the summer I got two very big surprises. The first surprise was from my father. He sent me a package in the mail that contained some clothes and record albums. It really shocked me because I never gotten any gifts from him before. It was an early birthday present. The package contained a black funky-looking shirt with large yellow polka dots on it. There were a few rock albums, too, and the only one I remember was of a group called, 'The Byrds.' I didn't care for the shirt or the music, but I was very happy. It was nice to know that he was thinking of me.

The second surprise was from my mother. She told me that Walter had found a house and as soon as everything was finalized we were going to move. I was simply overjoyed! This was music to my ears! We had been living there for over a year and by that time everybody had enough. We were going to live in a house again and I was going to have my own room. It would be just like grandma's house; a backyard, a front yard, and a stoop.

They had been looking for months and finally found the right place. My mother wanted to stay in Brooklyn and move to a neighborhood that was within walking distance to the schools. As soon as they got the mortgage she quickly registered us in another school. It was called St. Rose of Lima, and it was located on Parkville Avenue. In less than a month my sister and I would be in the new school. I was starting the sixth grade and Luann the fourth.

My mother and Walter took us to see the new house. We weren't ready to move in yet, but they were excited about the place and wanted to share that joy with my sister and I. The house was situated on a one-way street in the middle of the block. The neighborhood was called Kensington. My mother's brother Frankie and her sister Mary lived directly across the street.

The first thing I noticed was the front yard which was crowded with overgrown shrubbery and hedges. The house and the roof were both covered in dark grey shingles and the wooden porch was slanted. When we walked into the house there was a narrow hallway and a staircase. On the first floor there were three nice size rooms: a kitchen, a dining room, and a living room. The door in the kitchen led to a small porch overlooking the backyard. It was a dirt yard surrounded by a silver wiry fence and dominated by a humongous tree. Upstairs there was an average size bathroom and two other rooms on the left. One was a master bedroom and the other was a square smaller bedroom. The two bedrooms were separated by a steep staircase which led to the attic. Up there were two more average size rooms with low pitched ceilings. Eventually the room on the right would be my bedroom and my sister got the room on the left which faced the street.

There was no doubt that this place needed a lot of work but Walter was optimistic. He was very handy and my uncle Vito (my Aunt Mary's husband) was a construction worker. Together they had plans to turn this place out.

In the weeks that followed Walter spent all his free time preparing the new house and getting it ready for us to move in. He made the transition hassle free and by the middle of the fall we were ready to go. I was already enjoying my new school and soon I would be relishing in my new home.

One of the things I liked about St.Rose of Lima grammar school was that it was coed. I found the girls to be friendly, very smart, and some of my biggest fans. There were no brothers or male instructors, just lay teachers and nuns. They were strict and physically disciplined us whenever they felt it was necessary.

It was a large parish that had two churches, a school, a convent, a rectory, and a newly paved schoolyard. The upstairs church reminded me of St. Patrick's Cathedral in Manhattan. It looked magnificent with its high artistic ceilings and thick marble columns. The basement church was much smaller and plain looking. The schoolyard served two purposes: It was our playground during the week and a parking lot on the weekends for all the parishioners attending mass.

I made a lot of friends at school and having girls there for the first time changed the dynamics of the classroom and brought me out of my shell. I discovered that I had a natural ability to make them laugh, hence I was easily accepted and that made me feel good. I never disrupted the class like some of the other boys did; with their spitball antics or 'fart like' sounds. I wasn't a bully or the class clown and I never teased any of the kids, either. Instead, I used my charm and sense of humor to get on their good side and become their friend. I had a talent for mimicking the teachers and liked giving my classmates a show every time the opportunity presented itself.

In seventh grade I became very religious and spent a lot of time praying to my favorite saints. I frequented the basement church because it was quiet and peaceful most of the time. There were a few very colorful, life-size statues of saints which looked real and always fascinated me. There was one particular saint located next to the confessional that was most popular. The old ladies came in everyday to have an emotional conversation with her. Some knelt very quietly and caressed her feet while others stood there shaking their rosary beads at her.

The eyes on the statue appeared to be made of glass and no matter where you stood or sat in that church, it looked as though they were watching you. I wanted to know exactly how they felt so one day I made up my mind to touch them. As soon as everyone left the church I climbed up and placed my index finger into one of her eyeballs. It felt like the marbles I used to play with when I was younger. I wasn't impressed and quickly jumped down. Suddenly I had another idea. I knew if I could put a few small drops of holy water into her eyes she would definitely look like she was crying. Then the old ladies would see the tears flowing down the saint's face and believe that they were witnessing a miracle. They would get all dramatic and make a scene.

I looked around, once again, to make sure I was the only one in the church. This time I put one of my finger tips into the holy water and placed a drop in the corner of each eye. I backed away from the saint and realized I needed to wet the entire eyeball so it would come down the face like real tears. I wet two of my fingers in the marble basin, and then brushed them along the surface of both eyes. It worked! When I looked at her, this time, even I believed she was crying.

I then knew I had to get out of there, quickly. As I was on my way out the door an old lady was coming in. I recognized her as being one of the regulars; the quiet one who liked to caress the saint. She smiled at me and I mentioned to her that the saint was crying. She had a puzzled look on her face like she didn't believe me. I made an about-face and escorted her into the church. When we approached the saint I pointed to the eyes and showed her the tears. She stared at the statue in disbelief and then dropped to her knees screaming that it was a miracle.

When she finished praying she ran out of the church looking for others to tell. I hid in the confessional booth waiting for the show to begin. In fifteen minutes the place was packed and people were waiting on line just to get a glimpse of the miracle saint. Peeking from behind the curtain it looked like the geriatric ward for the spiritually connected. I was hysterical, bouncing all around inside the booth, and trying to control my laughter. It was an incredible mob scene!

Then, out of nowhere I heard a familiar voice telling the crowd to disperse. It was my homeroom teacher, a nun, and she sounded pissed. She knew it was a hoax and I needed to sneak out of that confessional booth right away. As soon as she turned her back I jetted out of the church. I ran all the way home thinking that they were going to expel me for my blasphemous stunt. Then when they got through with me, I would have to deal with my mother.

Everything was quiet when I arrived at school the next day. I was still scared that I was going to be found out, but nobody said a word to me about the miracle. Even if they did I was planning to play stupid. Finally after a few weeks I felt comfortable enough to go back into the basement church and say my prayers again.

Meanwhile, back at my house it was construction city. Spring had arrived early and they were tearing the place apart. Every weekend they mixed cement and laid down some cinder block. Next, they took away the rusty wire fence that surrounded the yard and replaced it with a cinder block wall that was four feet high. They built a small flower box in the corner around the base of that enormous tree, and then cemented the rest of the yard. The next day I planted some flowers and Walter placed my mother's favorite saint, St. Jude, in the middle of the flower bed facing the house. The house was finally finished and we spent the rest of the summer having barbecues and entertaining relatives. My sister and I were very pleased just to have our own rooms and now we had a wonderful backyard, too.

The summer was almost over and I was about to begin my last year of grammar school. I spent the last few weeks familiarizing myself with the neighborhood and finding a part time job. I found something in a local flower shop. It wasn't anything steady, but I liked hanging out in the store and learning about all the different kinds of plants. If there was maintenance to be done or a delivery to be made, then the owner put me to work. When I was ready to leave she would give me five dollars or a free plant. After going on a few deliveries I knew the neighborhood like the back of my hand. Another job I tried was at the supermarket where I packed the grocery bags for shoppers at the check-out counter. Some of the customers gave me a dollar and others just gave me a smile. I always preferred the flower shop because I made more money and got an education in gardening.

When I started eighth grade in early September the house was under major construction again. This time it was the front of the house. They were putting in new steps, a porch, and a black wrought iron fence. After they finished with all that, then they were going to cement the entire front yard. I was very disappointed when I heard them talking about more cement. I voiced my opinion and my mother said she had a surprise. They knew I had a 'green thumb' so they promised to put in two, nine-foot long flower beds, so I could do some gardening. When I got through with those beds, I had transformed the entire front yard into my own mini-botanical gardens.

Eighth grade was my final year in grammar school and my favorite. I thought it was going to be a difficult one scholastically because of all the tests in preparation for high school. But it turned out to be just fine. It was the beginning of my adolescent years and the start of something new. There were changes happening physically, mentally, and emotionally. Even my attitude and general disposition seemed to be going in different directions. I was in the middle of puberty and feeling overwhelmed.

I had a crush on a girl in my homeroom class and it took me three weeks to ask her out. I was very insecure when it came to my romantic side and I needed some coaching from her friends. We went to see the movie, 'Love Story', and I was still a little timid. I didn't know what to do. After an hour in the theatre I found the courage to hold her hand. In ten minutes my fingers were sweating. Then when I finally kissed her I felt dizzy because I was holding my breath the whole time. She had charisma and charm. I tried to impress her so she would be my steady girlfriend.

We were eighth graders now and had an advantage. We were the oldest students in the school and given a little more freedom. The teachers treated us like adults and encouraged us to think for ourselves. They engaged us in various projects and wanted us to explore our creative side.

My special project was a song by the Jefferson Airplane called, "We Can Be Together." It was the first rock album that I ever bought and one of my all time favorites. My plan was to play it in class and then discuss the meaning of the words. I knew the class was going to love this song because there was a curse word in it. It was subtle and I knew when I pointed it out to them they would definitely hear it. The teacher had a slight hearing problem and there was no way in the world that she would catch it. That was a good thing, meaning that I wouldn't get busted. I would be able to play the nasty part over and over again and make my classmates crazy.

When I got to class the next day I told the other students about the song. I told them they had to listen very closely and watch for me to signal them. The teacher placed the record player on a desk in the middle of the classroom and put the song on. I was standing right beside her and offered her the printed words from my hand. The sound was too low so when she looked away I turned up the volume. I wanted to make sure no one in the classroom missed it. While she was busy reading the words I motioned to the class that the nasty part was coming up. I wasn't worried that she was reading the original lyric sheet because the "F" word wasn't printed on it. And believe me; I made sure it wasn't there. When the nasty part came up only a few of the kids caught it. A couple of them chuckled but the majority of them missed it. I took the arm of the record player and placed the needle on the part of the song where the curse was. I knew the exact spot because I rehearsed it about twenty times the night before. I did that six or seven times until everybody was hysterical. Then they started to get rowdy and the teacher immediately stopped the record and shouted at them to calm down. She refused to continue until everyone was silent and back in their seats. Then she had me explain the meaning of the song and the reason why I picked it. I had no trouble interpreting the song in front of the class, but it was real hard doing it with a straight face. Anyway, I got an "A" and got over!

That year things were good. My mother and Walter got married and seemed content. Our financial picture looked better and my sister and I were doing exceptionally well in school. I became a teenager in July and my mother allowed me to grow my hair longer. I got to spend time with my grandmother and for my birthday she took me to her girlfriend's bungalow which was located on a beautiful lake.

In the same year I went to see my father a few times and even slept over his house once. He lived in a beautiful, one bedroom apartment, on West End Avenue, in Manhattan. The apartment was located on a high floor in a luxury building that had a twenty-four hour doorman. My father would rent a car and come pick me up at my house. When we got to his building they opened the door for us and then offered to park his car. They addressed him by his last name and checked the front desk to see if there was any dry cleaning or packages left for him. I was so impressed. When we got upstairs his wife Patti was home. She offered me a beverage and gave me a quick tour of the apartment. The first thing I noticed about the place was that it was impeccably clean. They had cushy wall-to-wall carpeting, brand new furniture, and fancy curtains, too. Patti was a collector of clown statues, and she had them meticulously displayed on a shelf along with some other knickknacks and photographs. It was more than obvious that she loved clowns and now it made sense why she married a comedian. I also noticed that there weren't any pictures of my sister and I anywhere in their apartment. My mother and my grandmother had photographs of us all over the place. My father had everything else in that apartment except a picture of his children. I couldn't understand why and it hurt me. I wanted to confront him about it but I was too afraid.

I remember the first time I slept over his house. Patti did everything in her power to entertain me. She took me along on all her errands, played cards, and even watched TV with me. She was always very cordial but I was just anxious to spend time with my father, alone. Sometimes I got the feeling that he was pushing her on me. I'm sure he wanted me to like her but it made me feel uncomfortable when he tried to convince me that she was the greatest woman in the world. As far as I was concerned my mother was.

The most important thing for me was that I was able to spend time with him even if it was just for a couple of hours. He enjoyed doing things with me that he knew I never done before. That year we went fishing on a big boat. Everyone was there; his wife, his cousins, his uncle, and his aunt. We were all the way out in the middle of the ocean and I was having a wonderful time, until I got seasick. Then another Sunday morning he took me out to Greenwood Lake with his manager so I could experience a motorboat.

Not long after our trip to Greenwood Lake he gave me the surprise of my life. I was at his apartment and we were having a conversation about his work and all the traveling he had been doing. He asked me if I ever been on an airplane or a vacation. I told him that his mother took me on my first vacation but it was in the Pocono Mountains and we went by car. Sounding surprised he said, "You never been on a plane?" I told him no. He immediately walked into the bedroom and picked up the telephone. I could see him pacing back and forth. I heard something about Boston but before I could hear anything else, he hung up the phone. He handed me my coat and said, "C'mon we're going for a ride on an airplane." I was flabbergasted! I looked at him in disbelief and asked, "A real airplane?" He answered me with a smile. On the way down in the elevator I asked him what day we would be returning. I thought we were going on a vacation and I wanted to let my mother know where I was. He laughed and told me that we were just going for a ride to Boston and back. He explained that I would be home in less than three hours. I had no idea that it would only take forty-five minutes to get to Boston. I was a little disappointed that we wouldn't be staying over night but was still glad just to be hanging out with him. As we approached the airport I could feel my heart racing. The last time I got this close to an airplane was when Walter took us. Now I was going on one of those big jets with my father.

When we entered the airplane I was greeted by a smiling stewardess. She let me peak into the cockpit and then directed us to our seats. The inside of the airplane was deceivingly small because from the outside it always looked so enormous to me. The aisles were narrow and the ceiling was low. We sat in the middle of the plane on the left side and my father, of course, gave me the window seat.

All of a sudden I felt the plane move. Then my father whispered, "Any second now." I felt a jolt and heard the sound of the strong engines. The plane accelerated down the asphalt runway causing us to bounce up and down in our seats. Everything inside the plane was rattling, and when I looked out the window again, we were leaving the ground. Our first few minutes in the air felt like one of the rides at Coney Island, except a whole lot better and much more intense. My father was watching me and gave me a big smile. When we got into Boston we walked around the airport for a while then boarded another plane and headed back home. That was it!

On the way back to Brooklyn I was a bit quiet. My father was busy driving and I just sat there in the front seat gazing out the window and coming down from a glorious day. The ride and the view weren't as impressive or spectacular as the one I just experienced a short time ago. I was exhausted and still praying that this day would never end. But I also couldn't wait to tell my mother about my airborne adventure. Then when I got through telling her it would be my grandmother's turn.

Saying goodbye to my father that evening made me feel very sad. I never knew when we were going to see each other again. The reality was that it could be a year or more. Something happened that day between the two of us. There was a special connection and a closeness that I never felt before. I had him all to myself and I felt valued. That's all I ever wanted; a little bit of his time and attention so I knew that he cared. I could see there were signs of hope and once again I thought we were back on the right track.

After our plane ride I didn't see him again until the following year. That's when he dropped a bomb on me. He told me that he was moving to Las Vegas at the end of the year. I was devastated and saw this as a major setback. That was like him moving all the way to the moon as far as I was concerned. He lived nearby and we hardly spent time together. Now he was moving all the way out there and I thought we'd never see each other ever again. I asked him how we were going to see each other. He reassured me that he would be in Manhattan often because of his work, and that we could get together then. I thought, maybe, he would be keeping his apartment in the city, so that he'd have a place to stay and also I would know where to find him. But I was out of luck again. When I asked him about that he told me he would be staying at some midtown hotel. I still wasn't happy.

It was so frustrating because I was a kid and the one doing all the work. I was the one making all the telephone calls to his house to see if and when we could meet up. And his wife answered the phone ninety five percent of the time. If I didn't make small conversation with her or ask her how she was feeling then all hell broke loose. She would tell my father and he would lecture me about showing respect. It was always something and they made me feel like I was a pain in the ass. I was always pursuing him and I hated that. He must have changed his telephone number a half dozen times, too, for whatever reason, and never even bothered to call to give me the new one. I tried not to be discouraged, but that night I felt like giving up. When I returned home I ran upstairs to my room and cried.

Once again my father vanished. One minute he was there, the next minute he was gone. I threw myself into my schoolwork and kept myself busy with rigorous academic training and test preparations. We were about to take our cooperative entrance exams and I had to do well if I wanted to get into a Catholic high school. That whole year revolved around those test scores. First you had to submit four schools of choice that you wanted to attend. Then, in a few months you received a notice from each of the schools letting you know if you were accepted or not. Even though I was well studied and an honor student, tests made me nervous. My mother already told me that public school was not an option. So I signed up for a study program on the weekends which would prepare me and help me reach my full potential. When I was done taking the test and everything was over, I felt confident that I had passed.

I started changing near the end of that school year. I became rebellious and began to challenge things in society. I don't know if it was my age or my insecurities, but I had a lot of things on my mind, and I was searching for some of the answers. One day in class that search caused me some serious ramifications.

It was just another day at school, a little warmer than usual for that time of the year, and the class seemed a bit restless. We were in the middle of an important lesson and the nun was explaining something on the blackboard. One of the other boys sitting next to me whispered a wise-crack about her and made a funny face. When the nun turned around she caught me laughing. She stopped teaching and demanded that I come up to the front of the room. I knew that I was in trouble but I didn't think it was going to be a big deal. I thought she would just have me apologize to the class for being disruptive. I had seen her reprimand some of the other students this way; first embarrassing them, and then just dismissing the situation. When I got up there she moved in very closely to intimidate me. Now we were standing face to face and she didn't tell me to apologize. Instead, she wanted to know the reason why I was laughing. I refused to give her an answer. She repeated herself, except this time louder. Once again, I stood there stone-faced and gave her the silent treatment. I don't know why I was being so stubborn but I didn't know what to say to her. Before I could even think of something she grabbed my hair and started pulling it with all her might. It hurt so much that it brought tears to my eyes. When she finally stopped I placed my hand on top of my head and let out a loud sigh. I was in pain and thought I might be bleeding. There was no blood but when I looked in my hand there was plenty of hair. I was so angry with her for treating me like that, and humiliating me in front of the class, that I blew the broken hair in the palm of my hand directly into her face. As soon as she realized what I was doing she started smacking me like crazy. I put my hands up in the air to protect my face and push her away from me. Somehow in the scuffle her head-piece loosened and almost fell off. I think that's what saved my life. Because while she was adjusting her habit I ran downstairs to the principals office and told her that I wanted to go home. I didn't expect her to understand or take my side because she was also a nun. I knew they lived together and were probably all close friends.

When my mother arrived at the school she stood in the principal's office discussing the situation for at least an hour. I saw the other nun come down and go in there, too. When she came out we both went home. My mother knew that I was traumatized and reassured me that they would never hit me again. I never understood why that nun wanted to make an example of me. I was always a good student and my grades reflected that. Besides, they never had trouble with me in the past. I'll never forget how I felt and how quiet it got in the classroom while all that was going on.

The next day at school was very uncomfortable. In fact, the remaining two months were. I noticed a change in some of the other nuns towards me, and I found it odd that this incident was never mentioned again. I was proud of my mother for taking care of it the way she did. I really liked that school, but now more than ever, I was glad to be getting out. It was unfortunate that it ended on such a sad note.

That June I graduated from St. Rose of Lima grammar school and thought I was free from books and tests for two months. Nazareth High School surprised me with a mandatory reading list to be completed before my arrival in September. I couldn't believe that they had the nerve to give me homework already. I swore that I wasn't going to read any of those boring books on my time off. I wanted to spend the next ten weeks doing what I felt like doing even if it meant just sleeping late everyday. I remember telling my mother that the kids in public school weren't required to do any reading over the summer. I thought I could change her mind or sway her into letting me switch to a public school. She knew what I was trying to do and said it was out of the question. I made up my mind to read one of the books and buy the cliff notes for the rest. They were not going to ruin my summer!

I spent the first few weeks of my summer vacation hanging out on the block and trying to bond with the other boys. There were a lot of kids my age and they all had one thing in common; they liked sports. They knew all the rules about baseball and foot-ball, and even enjoyed playing them for hours in the streets. They traded baseball cards and knew about the players and the teams that they were on. Even the girls liked playing ball in the streets. Everyone enjoyed sports except me. My sister was athletic and loved playing baseball. She knew a lot about the game and even had a uniform. That made things worse and I was embarrassed that they always wanted her on their team instead of me. I tried to learn but it was no use. I didn't have it in me. My father was never around to teach me how to throw a ball or even catch one. I was supposed to like competitive sports because I was a boy. I even bought baseball cards so I could learn the names of all the famous players. I did everything I could to catch up with the others. But those boys were playing sports for years. I was never exposed to any of them and by the time I moved into that neighborhood I was so far behind. I know it would have been easier to make friends if I was acquainted with sports at a younger age. Perhaps I would have been spared the harsh ridicule and teasing from the boys.

One day I made the mistake of working in the front garden while they were all playing on the street. They started laughing at me and calling me names like faggot, homo and queer. The harassment continued for a while and one of them physically threatened me. My mother and Walter were forced to go to his house and speak to his parents. That didn't help the situation because they had the same mentality as their son. From that day on I avoided hanging out on the block. And when I wanted to do some gardening, I did it in the backyard where none of them could see me.

At around the same time all this nonsense was going on I got a chance to see my father. This was our first 'get-together' since he moved to Las Vegas and needless to say I was very excited. When I got to his hotel room I was quite surprised to see an adorable little blond haired girl waddling around the room. My father casually mentioned to me that her name was Patti Jo and that she was adopted. He cautiously lifted her up onto the couch and caressed her little hand. Patti appeared from the other room, gave me a quick hello, and then tended to the baby. I sat pensively, observing the new addition to the Cooper family when I suddenly began to feel uncomfortable. I hurried into the bathroom to escape the intensity of the moment. I just stood in there pretending to be using the toilet and having a conversation with myself in the mirror. He never hinted at or even expressed a desire to adopt a child! What was this all about? And why did he want more children when he already had two? I felt jealous of that little girl and betrayed by my father. Jealous because she was already getting the things from him that my sister and I never got. She had his attention which we never had; from a man who wasn't even her real father.

What about us? We were his kids and needed love, too. Did he forget we were his "blood?" He never had any time for us and now he had all the time in the world for her. He was pushing us out of his life more and more everyday. In ten years time he changed his name, his wife, his house, and now his children. The harsh reality was that my father and his wife created a whole new family and there wasn't any room in it for me and my sister.

When I came out of the bathroom I was ready to leave. I felt like my world was shattered and all my past efforts were in vain. I didn't know when I would see him again and wondered if it even mattered anymore. I was angry at myself because I didn't have the courage to tell him how I really felt about things. He was the only one I was afraid to do that with. I thought it would jeopardize the little connection that we had and alienate us forever. At home I complained to my mother about him and that got me all worked up even more. In the middle of all that venting I realized he never gave me his phone number. This time I went from feeling hurt by his actions to incredibly angry with him. Something was bubbling up under the surface and I felt like I was going to explode.

Chapter Five

- Rebel Rebel -

That summer around the 4th of July I made friends with an older girl who lived down the block from me. She was a very skinny hippie chick who lived in a small cluttered apartment with her mother. I saw her one day walking along the street and smoking a joint. For some reason I felt drawn to her and wanted to find out what she was all about. When I approached her she seemed distant probably from all the pot she just smoked, but she engaged in a conversation with me anyway. A week later I saw her smoking again. This time I ran up to her like she was a long lost friend. Showing her hospitable side, she invited me over to her house to smoke a joint.

The first thing I noticed when I walked in the door was an indescribable foul odor. There were cats walking all over the house which explained that disgusting smell. She took me to her room and quickly lit up a joint. She handed it to me and I took a drag on it like it was a cigarette. She took the joint from my hand and patiently demonstrated the way it was supposed to be done. This time I did it exactly liked she showed me. I gazed around the room for a couple of minutes waiting for the feeling to kick in, but nothing happened. She explained that I needed to hold the smoke in longer in order to experience the full effect. Unfortunately I had to get back home so I convinced her to give me a couple of joints to take with me so I could practice.

The moment I stepped into my house I became paranoid. I rushed to my room and stashed the joints in the closet under the loose rug, then went downstairs to dinner. That night I listened by my door until I heard everyone getting ready for bed. When I was sure everybody was sleeping, I locked my door and placed my small fan in the window. I put a thick towel along the bottom of the door to keep in the smell and then I shut the lights. In complete darkness I lit the joint and blew the smoke through the fan. I was almost finished with it when all of a sudden my heart started beating faster. I lied down on the floor and closed my eyes letting this seducing drug take me on the ride of my life. This became my ritual every night from that day on. My new friend from around the corner would sell me loose joints that only cost a dollar each. I'd buy five at a time and that would usually last me a whole week.

Eventually I got comfortable enough to smoke outside. I used to sit on the benches along Ocean Parkway, a scenic six-lane highway a few blocks from my house, and get stoned. I started smoking cigarettes at the same time mainly because I wanted to camouflage the smell of the marijuana. I figured if my mother smelled it on me then I could tell her it was cigarettes.

When I wasn't hanging out on Ocean Parkway, I was home listening to loud rock music in my room. I'd be up there for hours blasting my Janis Joplin albums. She was the Queen of Rock and a self-proclaimed hippie, and in some strange way I identified with her. I would sing those songs everyday and drive my family crazy. My mother and I would fight, time and time again, about the loudness of the music. Sometimes even the neighbors complained. She never knew that I was stoned; she just thought I was being a typical teenager.

I was fourteen years old and the most important thing to me was making friends and being part of a crowd. I needed something to facilitate that, and pot and rock music opened the doors for me. I had discovered an alternative, besides sports, that would allow me to bond with and be accepted by my peers. In fact, after I became popular in high school, it didn't matter what the boys in the neighborhood thought of me anymore. I had changed and there was no way in the world I was going back to the way I used to be. I even decided that having a relationship with my father was not worth my effort anymore.

Frank was my first friend at Nazareth High School. We spent a lot of time hanging out in his neighborhood getting stoned. Frank and I met in the cafeteria every morning for breakfast and sometimes for lunch, too. The cafeteria became one of my favorite places in the school. I ate there twice a day for my whole freshman year until a McDonald's opened up around the corner; and then I became hooked on that place for about two years.

One day while I was eating my lunch, I was joined by another student. He wasn't eating anything and I assumed that he just wanted to sit and talk for a while. He sat directly across from me, not really saying much at first, but obviously peering into my plate. I thought he was hungry and wanted some, until he started making fun of my food. I guess he expected a response from me, and when he didn't get one, he stuck his fingers into my food. Instinctively, I picked up the plastic dish and pushed it in his face. He stood up to challenge me again and before I knew it, we were both being escorted out of the cafeteria by a very angry teacher. He dragged us out the back exit of the cafeteria into a narrow stairwell that led to the track. Within seconds, he pushed us against the wall and smacked our faces several times with a steady hand. Nobody ever hit me like that. When he was done disciplining us, he grabbed us by our shirt collars and marched us back into the cafeteria. My face was killing me for the rest of the day. But it didn't matter because I had decided I wasn't going to be bullied by anyone, anymore.

I started acting out more and more in school. One day I felt frustrated in my Spanish class and my teacher was in one of his usual arrogant moods. He called on me and when I didn't answer correctly, he made a snide remark. I didn't hear everything he said, but I knew it was condescending by the way the class reacted. I tilted my head down and under my breath I said, "Fuck you!" I knew he didn't hear me because everyone was still laughing. I almost got away with it until the class went from silly laughter to a provoking, "Oooh!" Someone heard what I said and told him. I thought, for sure, he was going to come down the aisle and pound my face like the other teacher did. Instead, he acted unbothered, snickered at me, and then just turned away. At that moment something told me that I failed his class.

Summer school was a drag and to make matters worse my class started right in the middle of the day. That made it difficult to go to the beach or plan anything else. There were no fans in the classroom and I thought I was going to die from the heat. I used to sit there looking out the window watching everyone else going to the beach. It was the worst. Needless to say, my summer was ruined, and my first experience at a public school was not fun.

My second year of Spanish was more terrifying than the first, but I made sure that I passed it this time. The teacher was surprised to see me back for another year of torture. He was even more surprised when I joined his soccer team. He was a dedicated coach and had a lot of patience teaching us the technique and the rules of the game. If he taught me Spanish like that, I would be living somewhere in Spain now.

It was that same year that I hooked up with an old classmate of mine named Joe, an Irish kid who I knew from grammar school. He was one of the more popular boys there, and the one who convinced me to go to Nazareth. He lived directly across the street from my school, but we never hung out then like we did when we were in high school. We were inseparable and did everything together. It's not like we had all the same classes, but we somehow managed to meet over at McDonald's for lunch, or outside for a cigarette, where we were often joined by his other friends. They embraced me and I finally became part of a group like I always wanted to be.

Joe and I always made plans to get together after school. He preferred that we meet in his neighborhood so we could get stoned and enjoy the long bus ride together out to the Kings Plaza Shopping Mall. This was the usual routine and our favorite pastime, especially when the weather was bad.

One day I decided to meet him at the mall. When I got there, I waited almost forty-five minutes for him. By the time he arrived, I was already pissed off at him for making me wait so long. We had a little argument, and after that, nothing went right. He wanted to eat in his favorite Italian restaurant, Sbarro's, and I wanted to smoke. He insisted that we eat first, and said he didn't feel like smoking outside in the cold. I assured him that we didn't have to, and that we could probably find a secluded place somewhere inside the mall to do it. Surprisingly he agreed. We checked out a few of the stairwells and even took the elevator up and down to see if the parking lots were empty. We were in the elevator, frustrated and about to leave, when I forced the doors open with my bare hands. I looked at Joe and said, "We'll make our own secluded place!" I wedged my skinny foot between the doors to prevent them from closing, and immediately lit up a big fat joint. Joe almost died, and started screaming at me, "You always have to get your way!" I flashed him a dirty look and dramatically whispered, "shut up, and just inhale before we get caught!" When I released the doors, we started to go down towards the main floor. The elevator bounced before coming to a complete stop, and the doors opened to a very impatient looking crowd. They were waving their hands frantically in front of their faces to clear away the residual smoke. We laughed about it on our way home, but still waited a couple of months before venturing back to the mall again.

That summer turned out to be the best and I spent more time in Joe's neighborhood than I did anywhere else. He introduced me to his neighbors and a beach called Riis Park. This out-of-the-way sand and surf was located on the Rockaway Peninsula in Queens, New York. It was a pain in the ass to get to, and no better than Coney Island, except that they allowed nude bathing on Bay 1. It was secluded, predominately homosexual, and always crowded. Only half of the bathers were nude while the other half were onlookers, Joe and I included, who came to see the sites. I made a big mistake going there stoned. I couldn't believe my eyes. I swore that I was hallucinating. By three o'clock it turned into a freak show, and there were a few people in the water that were pathetically huge. There was one old woman that had sun burnt breasts that were almost down to her knees. When I saw that I looked at Joey and rolled my eyes. We simultaneously burst out laughing. The best part of it was watching the onlookers and their reactions. This wasn't Europe where people are used to seeing that sort of thing. This is America, and when you take your clothes off in this country, especially on a public beach, you are going to draw a crowd no matter what your body looks like. When we got home we were still talking about it. Needless to say, we became regulars there for a while.

The next night we had plans to go to my grandmother's for my birthday. She called earlier in the week and said she had a surprise for me. I knew what that meant and asked her if I could bring a friend along. She never refused me and always welcomed my friends. I knew she was going to make one of my favorite dishes and I wanted Joey to meet her. It was time for him to experience some real Italian food, and besides, he was getting on my nerves bragging about Sbarro's all the time.

When we got there she greeted us at the door with a meatball on a fork. Joey found that amusing and thought she was really cool. We quickly took our seats and my grandmother wasted no time filling our plates. We were starving and devoured everything but the tablecloth. Joe's eyes lit up like a Christmas tree when he tasted her homemade sauce. I smirked at him and said, "I told you so!" We were stuffed, and while grandma was cleaning up, she told me to give him a tour of the house. I loved showing all my friends where I used to live. While standing in the hallway and reminiscing to him about my childhood, I could hear my grandmother's voice calling us for dessert. We rushed downstairs and saw her standing in the archway of the kitchen, holding a chocolate cupcake, lit with one white candle.

Shortly after their rendition of, "Happy Birthday," grandma announced that she was going away at the end of the summer. She grabbed my arm and casually asked me, "How would you like to go on another vacation with grandma?" I looked at Joey and this time my face lit up! I didn't even know where we were going yet, and already had given her my answer. When she said Miami Beach, Florida, I almost drop dead! I always wanted to go to a tropical place and experience a warm ocean. She said we were taking a bus instead of a plane, and asked me if I still wanted to go. Grandma knew that I couldn't sit still for more than ten minutes and figured I'd be crazed sitting on a bus for two days. Nobody knew me better than my grandmother did, and in one month, I would have her all to myself for almost two whole weeks. Now all I had to do was get my mother's approval. There was no way in the world that she would say no. We were arguing almost everyday and the situation in my house was getting worse. It would be a break for her and a much needed one for me.

I had turned into an argumentative teenager and gave my mother and Walter hell any chance I got. There were a lot of things that were bothering me and they made me angry and sad. I felt rejected by my father, resentful of my stepfather, and took it all out on my mother. There were issues with peer pressure and acceptance. And combined with all that, I had this incredible amount of energy and nowhere to channel it. It was difficult to relax and I felt anxious at times. I worried about everything and concealed a deflated self-esteem. There were high days and low days, depending on my moods. Some people thought I was on uppers because I talked so fast and appeared nervous all the time. That was one of the reasons why I liked smoking pot so much; it was the only thing that mellowed me out and slowed me down a bit.

Another birthday came and went and as usual; no card or phone call from my father. Deep down it bothered me but I had stopped letting it hurt me so much. The gift of going on vacation with my grandmother was all I needed to feel good. It was an opportunity for her to show me a good time and make another memory for me. It was also a change of scenery and a chance to get some peace of mind. Her offer couldn't have come at a better time.

Finally, it was here! The second vacation of my life, and all I kept thinking about was Miami Beach and all the fun I was going to have. We got up nice and early, had our breakfast and packed the last few things. The plans were to meet Aunt Mary and Aunt Rose before eight. Grandma never liked traveling alone, and it was the 'best' when her sisters came along. They were full of surprises and made the vacation a lot more fun.

As soon as we turned the corner, I saw a crowd of old people sitting on their suitcases next to a huge silver-grey parked bus. I knew that was our ride and felt compelled to walk faster. "What's the rush, what's the rush?" grandma repeated. "You'll get a window seat… it's early." I pointed to my aunts, who were standing in the street about two blocks away. You couldn't miss them with their typical bouffant-style hairdos and short sleeve flowery blouses. You could tell they were sisters. My grandmother was wearing her own version of Miami: milk white baggy shorts, a matching patent leather bag, and of course, a flowery top. So many flowers and we weren't even in Florida yet. By the time we got to the bus, I was drenched with sweat from schlepping those beat-up suitcases she made me carry through the streets. Grandma gave me one of her looks and nudged me to get on and find a good seat. I left the bags with the driver and flew up the stairs, walked halfway to the back of the bus and sat in comfort as the crowd started boarding.

Once we got out of the city and onto the major highways everything looked alike. I was so determined to sit by the window, but after doing that for a few hours, I was bored stiff. There were miles and miles of asphalt highways lined with cars, busses, and enormous trucks. Fast food restaurants were everywhere. That's all there was! It might have been the adventurous route, but it certainly wasn't the scenic one. Every once in a while I got a thrill when we passed a farm that had some cows and horses on it. That was beautiful, but they looked bored, too. There was nothing else for me to do but enjoy the ride and talk. And my grandmother always took an opportunity like that to tell me more of her stories. I could listen to them all day long, even if they were repeats. It was through those discussions that I got to know who she was and how she felt about things. She stressed the importance of family, over and over again, and spent her life keeping us together. "Family is all there is…that's life in a nutshell," she would always say.

The only way I knew we had reached Florida was when I saw the welcome sign. I waited almost two days for that and would have missed it if it wasn't for my grandmother. I don't know why they call it the sunshine state—we have plenty of sun in New York, too. And I expected to see palm trees all over the place once we left the Georgia border, but there were none. Some man on the bus told me that I wouldn't see any along the highway until we got further south. It turned out that he was right. I spotted several along the way, but nothing compared to what I saw when we made a left turn onto Collins Avenue. My face was glued to the window in awe as I watched these tall dancing trees welcoming us to Miami Beach.

We pulled up to the Lucerne Hotel on the corner of 41st Street and were greeted by a friendly staff just waiting to check us in. We didn't get our rooms for almost an hour and I kept myself busy by roaming around the lobby. The hotel was simply beautiful! I was staring at the fish in the fish tank and preoccupied with the fact that it was too late to go swimming that day. Suddenly I felt someone tapping me on my shoulder. "You ready, mister?" I recognized my grandmother's voice. "Lets go up to the room and unpack our stuff—then we'll get something to eat." She grabbed my hand as if she knew what I was thinking. "Don't worry, you'll have plenty of time to swim—this is our home for the next eight days." I swear my grandmother was a mind reader. She knew that I was a little bummed out and always had a special way of snapping me out of it. The next morning all those feelings were gone and I was ready to start having some fun.

Grandma said the magic words, "Let's go eat," and eat we did! Breakfast has always been my favorite meal of the day and they had a Continental buffet ready for us that was more than incredible. It was free and included in our package. That's all I had to hear. It wasn't everyday that I got the chance to eat my breakfast outside on a splendid patio in the middle of a tropical paradise.

My grandmother always had a hard time getting me out of the water in Coney Island. Well in Miami, it was almost impossible.

The temperature of the ocean was perfect, compared to what I was used to, and it was so clean that I could actually see my feet while standing in neck-high water. The August sun was a killer, though, and I couldn't stay out of the water for more than ten minutes without dying from the heat. I don't know how my grandmother did it; sipping hot coffee in the sun and keeping a watchful eye on me. Don't get me wrong, my grandmother loved the salt water, too; she always said it was the healthiest thing in the world. She never went under the water or out too far, a little dip was enough for her. She didn't know how to swim and she was worried about her hair getting wet more than anything else.

She let me stay in the water as long as I wanted and even rented a raft for me to play with. My mother was overprotective and never would have done that. My grandmother, on the other hand, was always good about giving me a little more freedom than her. Even as a child I knew that. And like a kid I took advantage of that by not getting out of the water when she told me to. When her friendly wave turned into a clenched fist, I had only two choices: listen or die. We've played that game many times before and grandma was always the winner. I knew she would never really get angry at me for something like that. That was just her little way of reminding me who was boss.

The relationship we had was 'magical' because we understood each other. We never had one argument. There were times I might have disappointed her, but I can only remember one time in Miami that she really got angry with me. I normally reserved acting out for school or my mother, but this time I did it in my grandmother's presence.

It was our fifth day in Florida, and we were patiently waiting at the breakfast table for my aunts to join us. Grandma was a little restless that morning and couldn't understand what was taking them so long. She sent me upstairs to their rooms to see if I could speed things up. They weren't there and I assumed they went down already. Unable to resist, I started playing with the buttons in the elevator. That's when the trouble began. It came to an abrupt stop which usually happens when you push the red button, but the alarm didn't sound off. I waited about a minute before pressing the emergency button again. Still nothing happened! I began to feel claustrophobic and to make matters worse there was no air conditioning in there. I felt like I was in an oven. I tried separating the doors the same way I did in the elevators at the Kings Plaza Shopping Mall. I forced them opened and let them close by themselves, again and again, to see if I could get the mechanism started. After five minutes I gave up and sat on the floor staring at the ceiling and thinking about my grandmother. She had such a nice day planned and I had to go and ruin it with something like this. I pictured her running around the lobby looking for me and worried sick. I stood up and decided to give the doors another try. That's when I heard a couple of voices on the other side of the wall. I called out to them and begged them to get help. "Please tell my grandmother that I'm stuck in the elevator—her name is Louise. She's in the lobby somewhere with my two aunts. You can't miss them; they all look alike and they have flowery kerchiefs wrapped around their puffy hair." I heard the man tell his wife to go to the desk for help. He stayed and consoled me until maintenance came. It took them more than a half an hour to get that carriage moving again, and now I had to face my grandmother.

I couldn't believe what time it was when I got back down to the lobby. I had been stuck in that box for only an hour. But time didn't matter anymore; the damage was already done. And I was very sure it was enough to aggravate my grandmother. A hotel worker took me over to her where she was sitting with my aunts in the dining room. When I sat down at the table they didn't even look at me. The expression on my grandmother's face said it all. I tried explaining to her what happened, but she just ignored me. She was pissed off and ended up giving me the silent treatment for most of the day. Grandma was not one to hold a grudge, but she made her point and I learned my lesson.

The next morning everything was back to normal except my skin. I was burnt to a crisp and grandma said I looked like a lobster. She had her own remedy for that and rubbed Noxzema all over my body. It eased the pain a little, but I still had to wear a T-shirt in the water. Then as soon as I came out, she made me stay in the shade. That was impossible to do at the beach, so the only other option I had was to stay by pool. It all turned out okay because I made a friend; an older girl from Connecticut who fell in love with my Brooklyn accent. I ended up hanging out with her the rest of my days in Miami.

The vacation was almost over and we spent the last couple of days sightseeing and eating in a fancy Italian restaurant on the strip. Grandma even took me next door to see the famous Fontainebleau Hotel where a lot of big stars entertained. It looked liked a palace and I wondered if my father ever performed there.

Before I knew it we were on the bus headed back to New York. That was the worst part of the vacation besides the incident in the elevator. I dreaded the ride home because I knew what to expect this time. I had hoped the driver would take a more scenic route so it wouldn't be as boring. No such luck! It turned out to be the same exact ride except in reverse.

It took me a few days to get back into the swing of things. Joe and I hooked up on Labor Day weekend and went shopping at the mall to buy some new school clothes. I couldn't wait to see my best friend again and get back to our routine. We celebrated with a joint, and then I gave him all the details about the trip including the elevator mishap. He didn't believe me when I told him that I wasn't smoking pot in there. I told him that I was too paranoid and would never take a chance like that, especially down in Florida. Besides, I had a lot of respect for my grandmother even though I could have used one on the bus. I was a daring teenager, but not a crazy one. We ended the day at Sbarro's, my treat, and made a little pact to go down to Florida as soon as we both graduated.

That semester was more of everything: more choices, more friends, more trouble, and more fun. I was wilder than ever, and by this time it was part of my daily routine to meet my friends at Mc-

Donald's for lunch. The fish filets and Big Mac sandwiches kept me going back, but it was more than just the food. Over at McDonald's we could let loose, smoke cigarettes, or have French fry fights without being suspended. It was a safe haven for me and my friends or so I thought.

One day we went to McDonalds as usual and it was packed with kids. Richie and I were lucky to find three seats. We sat there making funny faces at the kids sitting next to us while Joey waited on line to get our food.

Richie was a mutual friend of ours; a good looking Italian with an olive complexion, light blue eyes, and long wavy black hair. He was a knockout! I hung with him whenever I could which wasn't very often because he had a possessive girlfriend. Joe and I competed for his attention and I think we both had a secret crush on him.

We also took turns trying to impress him. I was far better at it than Joey was, and that made him nuts. By the time he came back to the table I had already decided to play a little joke on him. I gave Richie the eye so he'd know to play along with me. With a serious face I stated that we should try smoking some pot through the stethoscope; the one we used in the biology lab that morning. "It would make the best homemade pipe," I said. Joe gave me a puzzled look, but I could tell he was entertaining the idea. He needed a little more convincing and that's when I discreetly kicked Richie's leg. He quickly intervened and made like I had just proposed one of the most ingenious ideas of the century. Joe looked at him and said, "Who's going to take the stethoscope?" "Whoever can sneak it out, Richie replied, and then we'll put it back when we're done." Joe hesitated, stuffed some more French fries in his mouth, and then looked at both of us like we were crazy. We remained serious and pushed the idea until we finished lunch. Then, when we got outside, we started laughing so much; he immediately realized it was a joke.

At 7 PM that night I had the whole house to myself. My family just left to go shopping so I took the opportunity to play my music on the downstairs stereo. First I smoked a joint in my room to loosen up. Then I put on my Janis Joplin album and starting singing along.

Right in the middle of my concert the telephone rang. I never liked answering it when I was stoned. It made me paranoid and I always thought the caller could tell that I was high. Besides, it brought me down. The only reason why I answered it was because I thought it was Joey. He was expecting me to drop by his house that night and probably wondering where I was. On the third ring, I picked up.

"Hello Joey," I said confidently.
"Caputo," I heard a stern voice.
"Yes, who's this?" I answered with a silly giggle thinking it was my friends playing a joke.
"I better have that stethoscope on my desk tomorrow morning or else," he said demandingly. After hearing that tone I was sure it wasn't them. It took less than two seconds to realize it was the Dean.
"I know you and the other two guys took it for your marijuana kicks and I've already called both of them," he said sarcastically.
My voice trembled with fear. "We didn't take the stethoscope...I swear we didn't...we were only joking about it."

I was beginning to have my doubts, thinking that maybe Richie really took it and now I would have to bear the brunt of it all. Joey wasn't a thief, but maybe he did it to impress Richie. Anything was possible at this point. I was totally confused and pleading with the Dean to believe me. How did he find out? Did he really call my friends already? Did they blame me just to cover their own asses? My thoughts were endless and I couldn't think straight because I was still so stoned. I didn't know what to think, besides, my head felt like it was about to explode. Before slamming the phone in my ear, he said, "You better pray to God the stethoscope is there when I get in tomorrow morning."

Right after that, I called Joey. He picked up on the first ring. "Did he call your house, too?" I asked.
"Yes, ten minutes ago," he whispered.
"Oh God... Do you think we'll be expelled?"

This time he just gave me a loud sigh. I heard his mother in the background and realized he couldn't talk. As soon as I hung up with him, my family came home. Thank God my mother hadn't gotten that call was all I kept thinking. She would have killed me on the spot, and there was still a chance she might find out. Maybe that's why Joey couldn't talk; because his mother knew already. Suppose she calls my mother and tells her? I was starting to panic and ran upstairs to my room to think about what just happened. I made sure to leave my door opened so I could hear the phone ring, just in case the Dean called again.

I couldn't fall asleep that night because all I kept thinking about was the three of us in the Dean's office the next day. If I got expelled, all my mother's hard work would be in vain. She spent years in family court fighting with my father just to get our education paid for. Tomorrow it could all go out the window in seconds, for a stupid joke, and a stethoscope that I didn't take.

The next morning I left the house extra early. The Dean made me wait fifteen minutes before calling me into his office. "Caputo, get in here," he ordered. He gestured for me to sit down in one of the leather chairs positioned directly in front of him. I thought he was going to interrogate me again; instead, he just sat at his desk staring at me and intently listening to what I had to say. When I was through talking he left me there and told me he was going upstairs to check with the biology teacher.

Gazing around his office, I could tell he was a regular family man, a good husband and a dedicated father. After looking at the pictures on his desk, I thought his wife and kids looked familiar.

The more I stared at their faces the more I thought I've seen them around somewhere. I racked my brain for a few minutes and then it hit me! They were the people sitting next to us at McDonald's. I recognized his kids because I was the one making faces at them. That woman was his wife. She listened to everything we said then went back and told him. And it was easy for her to identify us because my friends and I always called each other by our last names. It all made sense now.

He startled me with his loud voice when he stepped back into the room. "Caputo, you're off the hook. Nothing was robbed...now get to class." I gave him a timid smile, and then ran out of the office bumping into my friends. They looked worried, and I winked at them to let them know that everything was going to be ok.

I don't think we ever forgot that incident. I know I never did. We were reminded every time we ate at McDonald's. What were the odds to be sitting right next to the Dean's wife and kids? Next time I'll make sure to keep my mouth shut especially when I'm in a crowded restaurant like that.

November ended on a good note. My mother and Walter hit the number using the first four digits of our telephone number. They were elated, to say the least, and it was the perfect time to ask them for another dog. They were reluctant at first, which was understandable; my mother promised to get me one as soon as we owned a house, and I reminded her that she was already three years overdue. She never went back on her word, so she talked it over with Walter and that's when Boots came into the picture. I found her from an ad in one of the local papers. She was a six-month old puppy; a mutt, half retriever—half boxer. When my mother first saw her she immediately refused and said the dog was too big. It took some begging from my sister and I, and a few friendly licks from the dog to change her mind.

Not long after I got Boots I met my first girlfriend. I met Joanna on my way home from school. As soon as she got on the bus I remembered her as being one of my old classmates from grammar school. We liked each other back then, but we were just kids and never took any of that flirting seriously. I could tell it was her sixteenth birthday by her candy corsage and the shopping bag overflowing with gifts. The minute she caught my eye, she asked, "What are you doing here?" "The same thing you're doing here," I replied. We both laughed and she sat down right next to me. I was surprised that she recognized me with my long hair. In the twenty-minute bus ride we talked about everything from school to family. I felt comfortable with her from the start and knew that I wanted to see her again. I told her that I was having trouble with some of my homework. When we got off the bus we exchanged telephone numbers and she offered to tutor me. I knew this was the start of something big.

Joanna lived around the corner from me in a two family house owned by her parents who were old-fashioned and strict. I think they liked me because if they didn't, they never would have allowed me to spend so much time at their house. However, knowing them, they might have done that just so they could keep a watchful eye on the both of us. I started going over there almost every night so we could do our homework together. Then we graduated to playing monopoly or watching television. There were plenty of times her mother turned me away at the door, for whatever reason. That used to kill me. Sometimes I had to go there with books and pretend we were going to do homework, just so we could see each other. If I wasn't at her house then I was on the telephone with her. I was constantly tying up the phone lines and sending my mother's bill through the roof. The only solution was to get my own private phone in my room. Within a month I got myself a telephone and everybody was happy. Now all I had to do was get hold of my father and give it to him.

Gina was Joanna's older sister. She lived in the downstairs apartment with her husband and baby daughter. Gina could empathize with us because she went through the same thing with her parents when she was dating. I really had to be in love with Joanna to put up with all their nonsense. We weren't allowed to hold hands while walking down the street because they said it made their daughter look cheap. They watched us like hawks. Everything we did had to be done on the sneak. There was no other way. God forbid if I kissed her in public; they would've chopped my head off.

Joanna was outspoken and daring. Persuasive was her middle name. One day we had made plans to go shopping and maybe see a movie. But she called me the last minute and said that she changed her mind. She had the whole house to herself and wanted me to go over there for lunch. I told her it wasn't a good idea because if her parents found out we would both be killed. She assured me that they wouldn't be home from work until six. When I asked about Gina, she said she took the baby to the doctors.

When I got there she was already waiting for me in the vestibule. As soon as she opened the door I could smell the food. Joanna was a great cook like her mother and surprised me with a delicious Sicilian dish. I munched that down in ten minutes and then I was off to her room to smoke a joint. That was my first time up there. It was in the attic like mine and facing the backyard. Her room was difficult to walk in because of the slanted ceiling and the queen size bed. There was one large window in there, a small closet, and no doors.

Before I knew it we were making out. I was enjoying the moment and in the middle of shifting gears when suddenly she pushes me out of the bed. She looked petrified. She gave me an order with such urgency that I'll never forget. "Hide in the closet...hurry... my sister's coming up the stairs!" I couldn't believe this was happening to me. My worst nightmare was becoming realty. She threw my clothes under the bed and I ran and hid in the closet. I was sitting on the floor in there, slouched over, and watching the drama unfold from behind her gowns and dresses. "Jo...Jo," her sister called out as she reached the top of the stairs. Now I could hear her. She was dragging something and coming towards the room. I thought I was camouflaged well, but then I realized my toes were sticking out. I panicked, and fortunately there was a large box of sanitary napkins that I used to cover my feet. Now all I had to do was sit tight and pray.

She came into the room wheeling a vacuum cleaner. It was one of those old floor model types that came with a dozen attachments. At first I thought she was there just to return it, but after listening to their conversation she had a different agenda. And when she plugged it in, I knew she was there to begin some serious cleaning.

They started arguing and dragging the vacuum cleaner around the room. It was bad enough that I could hardly breathe; now I felt the exhaust blowing in my face and thought I was going to choke to death. To make matters worse, her sister started vacuuming along the inside wall of the closet almost hitting my feet. That's when Joanna turned the vacuum cleaner off.

"I can clean it later," she shouted.

"No, it has to be done now," Gina said firmly. She turned it back on and that's when they began struggling with it.

Joanna turned it off again and yelled louder this time, "It's my room and I said I'll do it later!"

Then once again, defying her sister, Gina turned it back on. It was like a ping pong game; back and forth, on and off, almost a half a dozen times. That's when my girlfriend went berserk. She kicked the vacuum cleaner with such force that it sounded like an explosion.

"It's my room...now get out!" she screamed for the last time almost breaking my ear drums.

"You better have this place cleaned up before mommy gets home," Gina demanded, as she stormed out of the room.

It was finally over and Joanna told me to get dressed while she went downstairs to see if the coast was clear. I was so ready to get out of there; leaning over the banister, anxiously waiting for her signal. That queasy feeling in the pit of my stomach was getting worse. Then with a hand gesture and a whisper, she said, "Psst...now...go!" I flew out the door in under a second, practically breaking my neck. Finally, I was home free.

After my great escape it was clear that I had to make some serious changes. Joanna and I were spending too much time together, and I was missing my friends. Even Joey said we were like a married couple already. I decided to pull back a bit and not see her every single day.

It had been almost two years since I'd seen my father. My last experience with him was a 'shocker.' I was afraid that I would never hear from him again, especially since he hadn't given me his phone number. He promised me that we'd get together whenever he was in New York. I didn't believe him because even when he was living here, we hardly saw each other. Also, I knew it was going to take a lot more work on my part to track him down and find out what hotel he was staying at. I was getting tired of doing all the work all the time. I felt that if he was really interested in seeing me he could have at least called me, or better yet, have invited me out to his house in Las Vegas.

My grandmother should have been a detective. She always knew when her son was in town. She told me he was playing at the Westbury Music Fair, in Westbury, Long Island. I tried to persuade her to go, but she said it was too far and she didn't have any tickets.

"We don't need tickets, we're family. Besides, he should send us a limo?" I said.

"I don't know what's in his head...he's your father," she said. I could hear the sadness in her voice.

"Grandma... don't worry...pretty soon I'll have my license...and I'll drive the both of us out there next time, I promise." She looked at me and smiled.

I couldn't stop thinking about the conversation that I had with her. The more I thought about it, the more it upset me. He promised to call. What's wrong with him? I found it hard to believe that he had not been back to New York in two years.

The next morning I was still frustrated with everything and it consumed my whole day. It was a good thing that Joey was around that night. I needed someone to talk to and get me out of that mood. Instead, the more I discussed it with him, the more desperate I became. I told him that I wanted to see my father that night and that we should take a cab out to Long Island. At first he didn't think I was serious. Then he tried talking me out of it.

"We'll go tomorrow...you should think about it first," he said.

"There's nothing to think about...I made up my mind already... are you coming or not?" I said.

"It'll cost a hundred dollars...and I don't know how to get there," he said.

"I'm not paying for it...my father will. He'll pay for it when we get there...don't worry. We'll call car service instead...they'll give us a flat rate and they'll know where it's located. Besides, it's a very famous place." I said. He agreed and started to get undressed.

"Let me change my clothes and then we'll call the car," he said.

"No, No, we don't have time for that...look what I'm wearing...we have to leave now. I want to be there before the show begins, and you never know there might be a lot of traffic." I said.

The car came within fifteen minutes. The driver looked surprised to see two kids wearing street clothes and going to the Westbury Music Fair. "You know this is a forty-five minute ride without traffic, and a fifty dollar fare?" he said. We just shook our heads.

After that remark Joey gave me a look as if to say, you better know what you're doing. We were on our way and I felt relieved that my best friend was with me.

The first twenty minutes we hit a lot of traffic. We made small talk with the driver to pass the time, but I was still feeling anxious. I was staring out the window and thinking about my father again. He's going to be shocked when he sees my face. I hope he's alone this time so we can talk. I hate being ignored and I'm going to let him know that this time. After all, he broke his promise. But now he's got no excuse. I'll give him my phone number and hopefully he'll keep in touch.

"We'll be there in ten minutes," the driver said, interrupting my thoughts. Now I was getting scared. I grabbed Joey's leg and he almost jumped out of his seat. He was doing his own thinking and probably wondering how I talked him into this. I knew it was too late to start thinking about the consequences. What if my fathers not there? Suppose he's out having dinner? Who's going to pay the driver? I started saying my prayers because there was no way this guy was leaving without getting paid.

We pulled into a huge crowded parking lot. The driver wanted to know where to drop us off. I pointed to the far end of the lot where a uniformed security guard was standing. When the driver stopped, I told him who my father was and that he was going to pay for the fare. He turned around and gave me a dirty look. Then I spent the next five minutes arguing with him and trying to convince him who I was. He looked at me and said, "You go get your father and leave your friend in the car with me." "No problem," I said. Joey looked scared. I felt bad and ran over to the security guard who quickly escorted me through a silver door. There were a few employees inside and I asked them where I could find my father, Pat Cooper. One of them told me he wasn't there yet. I almost died. I knew Joey was sitting in the car with that guy and I didn't want this to turn ugly. I frantically explained to them that I needed to find him immediately because I had to pay the car service guy who was waiting in the parking lot with my friend. One of the managers went upstairs to the dressing rooms and brought down another guy. Finally, after explaining the whole story to him, he went out to the car without hesitation and paid the driver. I thanked him a million times.

He brought us back in and we waited a few minutes in my father's dressing room. I thought this guy was going to stay and baby sit us, but he left us there alone. The anticipation was killing me so I decided to give myself a tour around the room. There wasn't much to look at and it wasn't as fancy as I thought it would be. I expected to see some of my father's clothes around, like maybe a few ties and some shirts, but there was nothing that even suggested it was his room. I was still looking in the closet when he burst into the room.

"Mike, what's wrong?" He said, startling the both of us.

"Nothing Dad...I just came to see you." I said.

"Well, the people downstairs said my son was here looking for me...and you were upset...and needed to pay a car service guy," he blurted out as he plopped his clothes on the couch.

"I was...Dad, but the guy next door took care of it," I replied.

"What guy next door?" he asked.

"I don't know his name...some entertainer on the bill with you," I said.

"You're kidding me, Mike...you don't carry any money in your pockets...what's wrong with you?" He looked puzzled, and before I could answer, he pointed to Joey and said, "Who's this...your bodyguard?" (Joey laughed)

"He's my friend Dad," I chuckled. (Joey introduced himself and shook his hand)

"I can't believe you don't carry any money, Mike...between the both of you...no money. (Then he turns to Joey) What kind of bodyguard are you?" (Joey laughed again) My father shook his head from side to side, then motioned with his hand and said, "Mike, come with me."

We quickly walked down the hall towards another dressing room. It was very apparent that my father was not happy.

"Mike, I'm taking you to thank that man," he said.

"I did, Dad...I already did," I said making a face. As we approached the door someone was coming out.

"Hey Pat...how are you?" he said. I recognized him as the same man who paid the fare.

"Listen...I want to thank you," my father began in a serious tone, but was interrupted by his quick response.

"It's nothing Pat...you're welcome...don't worry about it," he said. My father looked embarrassed, reached into his wallet and said,

"No, no, absolutely not...thank you...you're a gentleman and I appreciate it...thank you...my son...Mike, I want you to thank this man."

"Thank you," I said in a gentle voice.

"He thanked me, Pat...he's a good kid," he said with a smile.

"I know... I know he's a good kid, but he's got to learn to do things the right way...he's going to learn to do them my way and not the way he wants to do them," he said in a stern voice.

My father was quiet on the way back to his dressing room. I felt a lecture coming on. It was bad enough that he already embarrassed me with that guy, now he was going to do it again in front of my best friend. When we walked in, Joey was still sitting on the couch and he looked bored. I sat down next to him while my father went to get ready.

"What time does the show start?" Joey asked.

"Pretty soon," I said. I saw my father go into the bathroom and I quickly changed the subject. "He's annoyed at me," I whispered, rolling my eyes. And when he comes out, he's going to start preaching, so get ready. Listen Joe, I'm sorry that I put you through this. I owe you a dinner at Sbarro's...I promise."

"It's okay, what are you worried about...once he starts, I'll leave the room...anyway Mike...where are we sitting?" he quietly asked.

"I don't know...I'll find out when he comes out of the bathroom...shhh...here he comes now".

"Mike, tell me something...your mother knows you're here?" he asked in a sarcastic tone.

"Nobody knows I'm here Dad," I said firmly. Joey took that as his cue to leave, and quickly left the room.

"Where's he going?" my father asked.

"I don't know...to look at the stage, I guess. Where are we sitting, Dad?" I blurted out, trying to change the subject.

"Sitting, he said quickly, as he adjusted his tie in the mirror. Right here in this room... (pointing to the couch) that's your seats." I gave him a puzzled look and felt stupid.

"I don't want to sit here while you're on stage, performing. I came all the way out here just to see you, Dad."

"Mike, you're out of line. You don't do things that way. I'm working...this is not a game...you're happy when the check comes to your house every week...when the doctor bills get paid...nobody thinks about me...that I got to go out there every night and make people laugh...I'm trying to make a living here, and you're worried about a couple of seats!" he said.

I never had seen him that irritated. I stood up and headed towards the door. "Where are you going now?" he asked.

"I'm going to find my friend and tell him that we have to stand," I said. I wanted to get out of there in the worst way and that was the perfect excuse.

"Sit down, I'm not finished," he demanded. "Listen Mike...if you would have called and told me that you wanted to see the show...I would've done the right thing. You embarrassed me... and embarrassed yourself tonight...because you weren't thinking.

"Have I ever refused you?" he continued.

"But...Dad...I didn't"..." he wouldn't let me finish.

"Next time you'll call me and do things the right..." That's when I cut him off and screamed out, "But I don't have your number, Dad, and never know what hotel you're staying at. You never call and let me know anything."

"You don't have my number?" he acted surprised.

"No I don't!" I said angrily. "Who am I going to get your number from? You change it so many times and never once called me to give me the new one." I said.

"Okay, Mike, listen...I'll give you my number and we'll see what happens from here on in. Now I got to go to work. Go find your friend and you can both watch by the side of the stage," he said.

"Okay, thanks. I just want you to know that I got my own personal phone number now. We'll exchange numbers later," I said as I walked out of the room.

I felt a bit overwhelmed that night, but very proud of myself. Not only because we were going to exchange phone numbers, but because I finally got the nerve up and spoke my mind. Even after all that, I somehow knew that things would never change.

The show had already begun by the time I got to Joey. Although it was a dark area, he found a good spot somewhere near the right side of the stage. We made the best of it and that's where we stood all night.

There was a comedy duo that went on first that reminded me of Jerry Lewis and Dean Martin. Joey pointed out one of them as the guy who paid the car service for us. The place was huge and they had a vivacious crowd that night. I couldn't wait till my father went on. Then they announced his name and the place went crazy. He opened his routine with, "These kids todaaaay…" he said, over and over again. They were hysterical already and he only said three words. I poked Joey every time he said something about me. He was working the room, pacing back and forth, and screaming his head off. They loved him, and all I kept thinking about was they should have heard him an hour ago back in the room with me.

When I got home my mother and Walter were watching the news in the living room. I went in to say goodnight and by the look on my mother's face, I knew something was wrong. My father had called the house screaming and blaming her for sending me out there. He carried on about the way I was dressed; that it was too casual for the Westbury Music Fair, and that it was a disgrace and an embarrassment that I had no money on me. His belligerent attitude continued until he successfully upset her, and then he hung up the phone in her face.

I went to bed trying to figure out what went wrong. All I wanted to do was see my father and it turned into a big mess. There was a weird vibe in the air that night, something uncomfortable that I never felt with him before. He treated me more like a nuisance than a son. He said one thing and his behavior said another. Nothing was accomplished that night, except that we did exchange numbers and I got to see him. It was quite obvious that I was more excited about that than he was. It took me sixteen

years to realize that, and it would take another sixteen years before I had the courage to tell him to his face.

A couple of months went by before I spoke to my father
again. Of course I was the one who called him, but this call was for
something different. My seventeenth birthday was coming up and
I wanted a gift from him. It had to be something that my sister and
I could enjoy even though it would really be my birthday gift. It also
had to be grand so that everyone could see that he finally bought
me something. My sister and I never got anything from him except
some albums and clothes he sent us one time when we were living on Dahill Road. I never understood why we had to ask him for
a gift. Why didn't he send something to the house or take us out
for the day like every other father would have done. He never
called us or even acknowledged our birthdays. That's something
I'll never forget. I was older now and it was too late for him to make
it up to me. But I finally had a house and a backyard. The only thing
that was missing was a swimming pool, and I was determined to
have him get me one.

It was never easy getting in touch with my father, even if I did
have his telephone number. Sometimes I would call Las Vegas for
weeks and never get an answer. Then when I did, his wife almost
always picked up the phone. We didn't have much to say to each
other and when I asked her if my father was home, she always
said the same thing; he's working. I never asked her where or even
pressed the issue, fearing that she would go back to him and say
that I was bothering her. Sometimes she would ask me if there
was something she could do. I always told her it wasn't important
and to just let my father know that I called.

When I didn't hear from him in a couple of days, I decided
to track him down myself. He gave me the names of the hotels he
frequented when he stayed in Manhattan. I called there everyday
to find out if he had checked in already. One day when I called, I
got lucky. They told me that he would be there the next day at
noon. I felt elated. Now, all I had to do was pray that he had some
time for me.

The next day I rang his room at noon. He wasn't there yet and I called back every fifteen minutes. I didn't want the people at the front desk to think I was crazy, so I disguised my voice every time I called. Finally, at 1:30 PM, he picked up the telephone on the first ring.

"Hello"

"Hi Dad"

"Mike...I just walked in...what are you clocking me?" he said jokingly.

"No...No... (I laughed.) I was just trying to get in touch with you...Did Patti tell you I called?"

"Mike, I didn't speak to Patti yet...I literally just walked in the door."

"Oh...well, I was wondering...how long are you going to be here?"

"I'll be here a few days, Mike...why...what's on your mind?"

"I'd like to come see you Dad and celebrate my birthday with you."

"What day's your birthday, Mike?"

"It's the eighteenth, Dad...two weeks before yours. Don't you remember?" I said, sounding surprised. (There was a short pause)

"How 'bout Monday?" he asked.

"No Dad, Mondays no good...I got a job now and..." he interrupted me.

"How 'bout tomorrow?"

"Tomorrows perfect Dad...Sunday is perfect...thanks Dad...what time? Where do you want to meet?" I said eagerly.

"Meet me at Patsy's Restaurant, around 2 PM...it's a nice place in midtown, Mike...in the fifties...call up...find out the exact address."

"Okay, Dad...do I gotta get dressed up?"

"Dress casual...Mike...presentable, okay? I'll see you at 2."

"Thanks...see you tomorrow...bye." (He hung up the phone.)

The first thing I noticed when I walked through the door of this fancy Italian restaurant was an autographed picture of my father hanging on the wall. He was already there sitting at a large round table by the window and joking with the owner. When I walked over to the table my father shook my hand and welcomed me.

"Did you have trouble finding the place?" he asked.
"No, Dad it was easy...only one train," I replied.
"You hungry, Mike." he asked.
"Yeah, I'm starved," I replied.
"Well, there's the menu...get anything you want." he said.
"Do they have baked clams, Dad?" I asked, flipping through the menu.
"They have all kinds of fish, Mike. You want baked clams...we'll get you baked clams." he replied. He turned to the owner and said, "I hope you have enough clams in that kitchen...my son's hungry...make sure you bring him a baker's dozen, okay." The owner laughed and motioned to the waiter to take our order.

Everything that day seemed perfect and most importantly I had my father all to myself. It reminded me of those days in Brooklyn when we used to meet at the Purity restaurant for lunch. Ten years have passed since our first meeting, and sadly enough, we were still in the same place with our relationship. I sat there disturbed about that and waiting for the right moment to ask him for the pool.

A little voice inside my head kept saying, "Now...now, ask him now Mike." Then it said, "Wait...not now...wait till dessert, stupid." I didn't know what to do and I felt like I had a lump in my throat. I knew it was getting late, and in less than an hour I would be on my way home. It was now or never. I excused myself from the table because I needed a few extra minutes to think. Why did I feel intimidated by him? He was my father. It wasn't about anything he said to me, it was more about his disposition that made me feel that way. He seemed preoccupied at times; like he was annoyed at somebody, or that something was bothering him. He never divulged any information about his personal life or ever expressed his feelings to me. We never had a real heart-to-heart talk, and God knows I was dying for one. It was always the superficial crap—the surface stuff. But that day I saw another side of him. That day his little lecture sounded like something from "Father Knows Best," the movie version.

When I returned, they were clearing the table and we were ready for dessert.

"What are you having, Mike?" my father asked.

"Mmmm…my favorite part…I'll have a cup of tea and a cannoli, Dad" I replied.

"Give my son his cannoli and I'll take a coffee," he told the waiter.

It was a good thing that my father started the conversation because I didn't know where to begin.

"So how old you gonna be Mike?" he asked.

"Seventeen, Dad… and I'll be driving soon, too…I got a job and everything this summer," I said.

"That's good…it's good to have money in your pocket, Mike, you're a man now…you're not a kid anymore," he said. I took a few more sips of my tea, and then the words finally came out.

"Dad, I was wondering…being that I'm working the whole summer… and I can't get to the beach…if you could buy me a pool… ya know…as a birthday gift." He got quiet for a few seconds, like he was thinking about it, but he didn't give me an answer right away. His mood seemed to change and then he spoke.

"Let me ask you something, Mike. Did they ever teach you in school how to speak on the telephone? (He paused) Didn't your mother ever teach you any manners," he said sarcastically.

"What are you talking about, Dad?" I asked.

"When you call people on the telephone, anybody, do you know the right way to speak?" he emphasized.

"Yes, I do," I answered.

"Well how come when you call my house, you don't know how to speak to my wife Patti?" he asked.

"I never spoke badly to her," I said.

"When you call people on the phone, Mike…the first thing you're supposed to do is ask how they're feeling…not… is my father there or put my father on the phone," he stated.

"I never did it like that, Dad, I swear...I don't have anything against her," I said. He saw that he was upsetting me and then out of nowhere he says,

"Don't worry Mike, you're gonna get your pool...I just wanna know when you're gonna learn some manners? (He paused to take a sip of his coffee) How much do you need for the pool?"

"Five hundred dollars, Dad" I answered. (He sipped his coffee again)

"All right...next week I'll have Patti send a check to the house. Look for it in the mail...okay," he said.

"Okay Dad, thanks," I said.

Then he stood up and said, "You ready?" "Let's go!" I knew it was time to say goodbye.

As soon as I got home, I burst through the door screaming, "I got my pool...I got my pool!" My family was happy for me and promised to take me out to a store on Long Island to pick it out. Walter already measured the backyard and said he had plans to build a cement deck halfway around the pool. Everything was in place and all I had to do now was wait for the money.

The check took forever to come and I couldn't understand why they just didn't send it express mail. There was a disturbing note enclosed with the check that read: Here's the money for the pool, God Bless, Pat and Patti. I couldn't believe it! There wasn't Dad or love written anywhere on that paper. She even left out the words happy birthday. I wanted to mention it to my father, but I knew it wouldn't do me any good. It took me seventeen years to get a gift out of him and I wasn't going to let her spoil it on me.

We picked out an average size oval-shaped, four-foot swimming pool. It took Walter a couple of days to get everything ready. But when it was finished it looked magnificent. It was mine and I couldn't wait to jump in. The night before we officially opened it, I sat on top of the deck just looking at it. It brought back beautiful memories of the fun we used to have at Casino pool. It also reminded me of when we lived on Dahill Road, and I used to stare out the window wishing that someday we would have a pool like those kids next door.

It was getting late and I knew there was one more thing that I had to do before going to bed. I went downstairs to the basement and took a flashlight and a couple of long nails back out to the pool. I took one of the nails and meticulously scraped it on the outside metal frame of the pool inscribing the words: Happy Birthday, Love Dad, July 18, 1974.

Chapter Six

- Oh Father -

Later that month Walter's mother, Mrs.D, came to live with us. She reminded me so much of my grandmother because of all the cooking she did. She and my grandmother quickly became friends and they used to exchange recipes all the time. One day while my grandmother and I were having one of our heart-to-heart talks, she brought up Mrs.D and made a casual remark.

"So now you have a new grandmother living with you." I was a bit surprised and quickly answered her.

"I might have a new pool, a new house, and even a new job, but I will never have a new grandmother." She got quiet as I continued to explain. "I refer to her as Mrs. D because I have only one grandmother, and that's you. I will never call anyone else grandma and no one will ever take your place." After a few minutes she was back to her old self and she never brought it up again.

I never believed in using the titles: mom, dad, or grandma loosely. If they weren't my blood relatives, then they were just 'step family' to me. Walter was my stepfather and I never called him dad, even though he was more of a father to me than my real one was. Patti was my stepmother and there was no way in the world I was going to call her mom. Neither one of my parents ever pressured me into calling their spouses mom or dad. And even if they did, it never would have happened.

I was now in my senior year of high school. Everyone was planning to go onto college and I was probably the only one in the school that wasn't. Joey was thinking about becoming a priest which came as a big surprise to me because he was never religious. He started hanging out with a different crowd and we slowly grew apart. We were still friends and had plans to go to Florida after graduation, but I knew it wasn't going to be the same.

Joanna and I became more serious, and I surprised her with a pre-engagement ring for her birthday. When her parents found out they called a meeting with my mother and Walter. My mother wasn't surprised and I thought that she handled them very well. By the time Joanna's parents left my house they made a couple of friends, changed their tune, and told their daughter that she could wear the ring.

Not long into my senior year I made an appointment to see a doctor. My throat was killing me and it was hoarse all the time. My grandmother's remedy—gargling with salt and water—wasn't working anymore. The specialist diagnosed me with small growths on my vocal cords. He said that my condition wasn't life threatening and that it was common among teachers, preachers, and singers. He suggested that I rest my voice and cut out the cigarettes. He told me to come back in a couple of months for a follow up.

I couldn't wait to get out of that office. I had received bad news and in addition to that I had to lay out $175.00 dollars. My regular doctor and dentist automatically forwarded the bills to my father, but specialists wanted the money upfront. I made a copy of the bill and sent it certified mail with a return-receipt to my father's house. I sent everything to their house that way, including birthday cards, Father's Day cards, and even Christmas cards so they could never say that they didn't get them. That was the best advice my mother had ever given me when it came to dealing with my father and his wife.

Before I got on the train to go home I bought the newspaper. I sat there thinking about what the doctor had said as I flipped through the pages when I came across my father's picture. He was playing at the Copa again for a couple of weeks. I was hoping to see him perform and this time I wanted to take my girlfriend and a couple of friends. I hadn't seen Richie since he left Nazareth H.S. and we had been meaning to get together for the longest time. This was the perfect opportunity. Now all I had to do was find out what hotel my father was staying at and then ask him if I could go.

As soon as I got home I called the same midtown hotel that he had stayed at the last time he was in town. They told me that he was checked in, but he wasn't in his room. I didn't want to make myself crazy calling all night because I knew he was going to be around for a while. The next morning I called him from school.

"Hello, hello." He sounded tired.
"Dad, it's me."
"Mike, where are ya?"
"I'm in school, Dad. I saw your picture in the papers...you're at the Copa?"
"Yeah, I've been workin a lot Mike...gotta grab it while I can... how ya feelin? Is everything okay?"
"Yeah, everything's fine Dad...listen...I want to come see you at the Copa again,"
"What night works best for you, Mike?"
"It's up to you, Dad...any night's fine,"
"Let's make it Friday, Mike...Saturday's too crazy... all right?"
"All right...Dad...can I bring a few friends with me?"
"How many Mike?"
"Three...Dad, I want to bring my girlfriend and another couple. Is that okay?"
"All right, that's fine. Come a little earlier, Mike, so I can get you and your friends a good table."
"Okay...thanks, Dad. I'll see you Friday night."
"Okay, bye."

When I called Joanna and told her that we were going to the Copacabana to see my father, she got so excited. Richie and Cathy wanted to rent a limo to take us there so we could make a grand entrance. I could imagine the look on my father's face if he saw me pull up in one those things. He definitely would've joked about it on stage, and then I never would've heard the end of it. I told Richie it wasn't a good idea and that it was better we go in his girlfriend's car.

Later that night I went to Joanna's house and she came to the door crying. I took one look at her and knew that her parents wouldn't let her go. They didn't want her going to a nightclub in Manhattan and coming home late. I pleaded with them and told them that we'd be traveling by car, but they still wouldn't budge. Joanna had her heart set on going and I was looking forward to introducing her to my father. Now I had to think about taking somebody else. The only other girl I wanted to bring was my good friend Arlene, and if she couldn't go, then I'd have no choice but to go alone. I was determined not to let that happen. After all, I told my father that I was going with my girlfriend and another couple; I didn't want him to think that I couldn't get a date.

Richie and Cathy picked me up at Arlene's house. We were all formally dressed and raring to go. I couldn't wait for them to hear my father. Everyone was familiar with his material, except Arlene. Richie and Cathy were Italian and their parents had all his albums. Arlene was Irish and never even heard of him. The only thing she knew was that I had a famous father.

For most of the ride the topic of conversation was about my father. Cathy talked about him being rich and said that I had to be, too. I was not a bit surprised by any of her comments because I had heard them a million times before while growing up. It was partially my fault because when I was young I went around telling all the kids in the neighborhood that my father was a famous comedian. I was proud of him and wanted to let them know that my father had records out and was on television. That innocent bragging turned out to be a double-edge sword which followed me every where I went. When I was ten years old they wanted to know why he didn't buy me the best five-speed bicycle in the store. When I was a teenager they wanted to know why I didn't live out in Hollywood in a mansion. There were plenty of times that I didn't know what to say and had wished that I had never opened my mouth. Arlene could tell that I was getting uncomfortable so she purposely changed the subject.

"What kind of food do they have there?" Arlene asked.
"All kinds from what I remember. As long as they have my baked clams I'll be happy," I said."

We were almost half way there waiting at a light when some-body alerted us that we were getting a flat. Richie immediately pulled over and checked it out. He said it looked bad and that the tire had to be changed. It was a good thing we weren't still on the highway or stuck in the tunnel somewhere. I felt bad that he had to change the tire because if it was up to me I would have driven that car with a flat. My main concern was to get us there on time and now I was beginning to panic. The last thing I wanted to do was embarrass my father or piss him off. Luckily, it took Richie less than twenty minutes and we were back on the road.

When we entered the Copa the main room was packed and exactly as I remembered it, stage and all. I went over to one of the waiters and told him that I was Pat Cooper's son. He escorted us to a reserved table in the center of the room and left us with the menus. My friends sat there in awe, looking around, and engaged in a con-versation about the décor of the place. From where we were sitting, I could see the same exact table that I sat at when my grandmother took me there years ago. It brought back beautiful memories of the night when I first saw my father perform. Now, here I was almost a decade later having dinner with my friends.

The flickering of the lights brought the orchestra to life. It was show time and I wondered where my father was and if he knew that we were there. We ordered our food and then angled our chairs to get the best possible view of the stage. Then out of nowhere my fa-ther appeared,

"Are they taking good care of ya, Mike?"
"Hi Dad…yeah, we're having a great time. When do you go on?"
"In a few minutes…as soon as I get the signal,"

The next thing I knew the crowd started clapping, and he was frolicking around on stage to some familiar Italian music. In ten minutes he had them hooked. Even the musicians and the waiters couldn't keep a straight face. Arlene nudged my arm every time he said something about me. Richie and Cathy were rolling on the floor. I knew his routine by heart and I still almost pissed my pants. My friends had to stop eating because they were laughing so hard. We were all in stitches for over an hour.

After the show a photographer approached the table and asked us if we wanted to take a picture. I definitely wanted one and didn't think my father would mind being that he got me one the last time. Besides, none of my friends brought a camera and I wasn't going to let this moment get away.

When we were getting ready to leave I went to find my father to say goodbye and thank him for a great night. I took my friends to his dressing room where they officially met him and his wife. We only got to talk a few minutes because they were leaving, too. On our way out we all got separated in the crowded lobby. As I walked through the doors I could see there were plenty of cabs eagerly waiting for the crowd of people exiting the club. Richie went to get the car and left the girls standing by the curb talking with me. My father went back inside to speak with somebody and Patti waited for him inside the lobby.

Unexpectedly, one of the cab drivers struck up a conversation with us. He had seen my father coming out of the Copa with us and wanted to know if we were related to him. Arlene told him that I was his son. He got so excited and started carrying on like a kid; telling me that his whole family loved Pat Cooper and that his parents were his biggest fans. Then he begged me to get him an autograph. I never encountered such a dedicated fan before and in some strange way it made me feel good. The next thing I knew I was back in the lobby looking for my father with a pen in my hand. Patti saw me looking around and thought something was wrong. I made the mistake of telling her that somebody wanted an autograph. She quickly took a cocktail napkin out of her purse and proceeded to sign my father's name. Then before I could think about it any further, she hurried me back outside with the bogus autograph. I handed the napkin to the cab driver and couldn't even look him in the eyes. I heard him say 'Thank You,' as I quickly jumped into the car with the girls. On the way home all we did was talk about the show. I was too embarrassed to tell any of my friends what Patti had just done.

I couldn't fall asleep that night and I began to think about the cab driver. I'll never forget how his face lit up when I handed him what he thought was my father's autograph. I saw another side of Patti that night—a deceitful side. I was very bothered by her actions and it made me rethink a lot of things. I knew I didn't like her anymore, that was a given, but it was more than just that. I couldn't trust her. The irony of the situation was that I had never even seen my father's handwriting or his autograph. My father never filled anything out. Patti always handled all of his correspondence. What she did to that fan was cold. She couldn't wait to get rid of him and anybody else that might get too close to my father. It was obvious that she had been treating me the same way my whole life. She might have been more subtle when dealing with me, but now she was beginning to pick up speed and showing her true colors. I realized that night that she was the one standing between my father and I.

The next day I had my follow up with the throat specialist. He was not pleased when he looked down my throat. I'll never forget the tone in his voice. He told me if I didn't stop smoking pot and cigarettes that I would end up with throat cancer. He scared me so much that after leaving his office I made a promise to myself to give them both up.

That year my father wound up being in town a lot. I tried to see him as much as I could and one day we met at Patsy's restaurant. It was one month before graduation and less than two months before my eighteenth birthday. I had plans to ask him for a combination gift this time, being that I had two important days to celebrate.

The conversation in the restaurant that day was like no other and only the beginning of what was to come. It started out on a flat note when he made a remark about his wife and kid going to Mc-Donald's in his Rolls Royce. I couldn't understand why he would even mention something like that to me. It was almost like he was trying to rub it in. He spoke a little bit about how life was different in Las Vegas as compared to New York, meanwhile never once inviting me out there to see for myself. I let him do most of the talking because I was waiting for the right moment to ask him for my gift. I knew exactly how much I needed, but as usual I wasn't quite sure of when or how to ask him for it. When I saw the bus-boy preparing our dessert, I knew it was now or never. On his way over to the table the waiter dropped my cannoli on the floor, and I took that as an omen.

"Dad, I'm gonna be graduating next month and I was wondering if you could help me out with some money towards a used car." He stayed quiet and just listened while I made my pitch. "Dad, I'll definitely have my driver's license by my birthday and it'll be like two gifts in one...if you could help me out a bit." He slowly turned his body to one side and then crossed his legs. I recognized the body language and knew something was up. He made me so nervous that I found myself squeezing my hands under the table as hard as I could. I got used to him not answering me right away, but I never got used to the guilt he made me feel for asking. Besides, this time I had a funny feeling that he was going to say no.

"What's wrong with your throat?"
"I have a nodule...like a little node on my vocal cords." He looked at me like he didn't believe me.
"I got all these bills coming to the house from specialists and you seem fine, Mike...just gargle with salt and water and cut out those damn cigarettes."
"But Dad it hurts, and they actually found a small growth down there."
"Oh, c'mon Mike, your mother would send you to the doctor even if you had a hangnail, for Christ's sake." I was shocked

and he wasn't finished yet. "Well, what are you going to do when the money stops? The party's over in two months...my friend."

"What are you talking about, Dad?"
"Eighteen...you'll be eighteen in a couple of months. Tell your mother to read her contract. "At that moment, I saw a side of him that I had never seen before. Why was he telling me this crap? "Yous only know me when yous want something. If you had my parents you'd still be riding a bicycle. Go out and work for it like I did."

"But Dad I am working...and a car's a lot of money, and I have to pay insurance, too. Why do I always have to ask you for a gift?" He stayed quiet and allowed me to speak my mind. "I never had to ask my mother for a gift, or grandma, or any of my relatives for a gift. It was always there, Dad. Every birthday, every Christmas, every occasion...my sister and I always got gifts from them. And even if I do ask...is that really so strange when kids ask their parents to buy them something? All my friends get things from their parents and they never have to ask. Why do you make me feel guilty Dad, and why do I have to beg you all the time? I don't understand that Dad...I just don't understand you!"

We left the restaurant rather abruptly and I thought by some lucky chance we might go back to his hotel room. I was on a roll and wanted to talk some more. Besides, he didn't answer any of my questions. The only thing he wanted to know when we came out of the restaurant was how much I needed for the car. I told him that I could get a decent one for around two or three thousand dollars. When we got to the corner he paused for a second, then turned to me and said, "You're getting one grand, Mike, take it or leave it."

I didn't return home with the same excitement that I had the last time when I got the money for the pool. There were different things on my mind this time, and I left him that day feeling terrible about myself. I mean, I was grateful that he was going to send me something and happy to see him, but it wasn't worth all that song and dance he put me through to get it.

As soon as I walked in the door my mother knew something was wrong. I told her the whole story and what he said about their divorce contract. She explained that he had to pay child support for me and my sister until we turned twenty one, whether he liked it or not. In a month, we ended up in the lawyer's office. I was having flashbacks when I walked in there because it reminded me of all the times we spent in family court dealing with the same nonsense. It was always a long drawn out ordeal, and it never ended pretty. It turned out that my mother was right. He had to support us for another few years with one exception; once we graduated high school he was no longer responsible for our education. He did have the option to pay for our college tuition. When my sister and I asked him, he declined.

My mother threw a fabulous graduation party for me in the backyard. The whole family came to celebrate my academic achievement. That weekend I made a call to my father in Las Vegas. I got lucky that day; he was home and answered the phone.

"Hello."
"Hi Dad...wow...I didn't expect to find you there."
"Mike, I live here...remember?" he said sarcastically. He paused for a few seconds and in the same tone he said, "Your checks in the mail...don't worry, its coming." I was taken aback by his comment and insulted.

I replied, "I'm not worried, Dad. I'm not calling for that...I got the check, already. I'm calling to say, "Thank You," and I wanted to see if we could meet before or around the time of our birthdays."

I was planning to surprise him with one of my graduation pictures. I thought, maybe, he would hang this one on his wall. But he seemed reluctant to meet with me and said that he would be too busy in the month of July. When I got off the phone I felt a little confused. Maybe he needed some more time to cool off, or maybe he thought I was going to ask him for something again. Whatever it was I tried not to let it bother me.

At the end of August I quit my part time messenger job. I wanted to keep my promise to Joey and go on that Florida vacation we both had planned. I knew when we returned I would have to buckle down and look for a full time job.

The first few days of the Florida trip were a nightmare. Joey made all the arrangements and we ended up in some awful hotel in Fort Lauderdale. As soon as we got to the room we unpacked some of our things and then went for a short walk on the beach. We didn't say anything to each other about the place, but I knew Joey wasn't happy either. At first I skirted around the issue because I didn't want to hurt his feelings. Then I just couldn't hold my tongue any longer.

"Joe...you like this place?"

"It's not what I expected," he answered.

"It wasn't like this a couple of years ago when I went with my grandmother."

"What can we do Mike? We're stuck here for three days until we go to Miami," he said shrugging his shoulders.

"Oh no we're not...I saw dead cockroaches in the bathroom. I'm not sleeping in that bed. You saw the floor...all filthy with sand...and that big moth that you had to kill. They probably haven't cleaned that room in weeks...Joey...I'm not staying here another minute," I said defiantly.

He gave me a puzzled look and asked, "What are you planning to do now?"

"I'm going to tell them that I have a family emergency and that I have to leave the hotel immediately."

"You're crazy Mike. Suppose they don't believe you."

"They have to let us go... I'll tell them it's a matter of life and death. Don't you worry...just let me take care of it. I'll be very dramatic... and they'll believe me. Go upstairs to the room and make sure everything is packed. Then I'll come get you."

"How are we going to get to Miami?" He asked.

"I don't know...we'll rent a car or walk if we have to. I'm not staying here tonight, Joey. If you want to stay then you can." He knew he was getting on my nerves.

Then finally he said, "I'll call my sister in Miami. She's here, too…maybe she'll come and get us."

"Okay, go call her and I'll take care of the rest."

As soon as we got back he went upstairs to the room. I went to the men's room in the lobby to sprinkle some water around my eyes to make it look like I was crying. That brought back memories of my mischievous days at St. Rose. Then I marched over to the front desk and gave them an academy award winning performance. The hotel manager worked out something with our travel agent and we were out of there in less than an hour. Joey's sister and her boyfriend came and drove us to our hotel in Miami, which turned out to be gorgeous.

Right after I returned from Miami I landed my first full time job at a local bank in the Brighton beach section of Brooklyn. It was a small busy branch and I was a bank teller. The hours were good and the location was perfect. I quickly learned about finance and accounting. The experience and work ethics that I got from that place were highly beneficial in every other job that followed. My mother's perseverance with regard to our education and getting a diploma proved to be an invaluable asset that was already paying off.

With the money my father had sent me I bought my first car. It was a used metallic green Chevy Camaro. I loved that baby! It cost exactly one grand and the insurance was $350 a year. I got a good deal from Walter's son who owned an auto mechanic shop at the time. He lived with us for a while after he came back from Vietnam. It was very convenient having somebody in the house that was a wizard with cars. He did everything he could to keep my eight year old machine running in optimum condition. After ten months I had to get rid of it because it was draining my bankbook. One week it was the brakes, the next week the transmission went, and then it was the tires. It turned out to be a lemon.

A few weeks later my life would change forever with an unexpected trip to Manhattan Beach. A friend who lived around the corner from me suggested that we explore some of the other fun beaches in Brooklyn. His name was Ronnie and he had lived in my neighborhood his entire life. I used to see him walking his big German shepherd dog up and down the block. One day we started talking and became friends. He had a beautiful second hand car that his parents bought him and we used to travel everywhere in that thing. The first place we went to was Riis Park. He never knew about the nude bathing on Bay 1 and I just had to show him some of the sights. Then he took me to Manhattan Beach and I was blown away!

We got there in twenty minutes and spent a half an hour riding around this exclusive neighborhood looking for a parking space. I lived in Brooklyn all my life and never knew this beautiful area existed. As soon as we approached the entrance I noticed that there was no boardwalk. It was the smallest beach I've ever been on and the most crowded.

From a distance I could hear the disco music blasting, but when we got closer I couldn't believe my eyes. This was a voyeur's paradise and there was enough eye candy there for everyone. I gave Ronnie a look like we just landed on another planet. I never had seen so many beautiful men, muscles, tattoos, and gold chains in my life. The girls were hot, too; parading around in their skimpy bikinis and flirting with the guys who were also busy showing off their bulges and physiques. Everyone seemed to know each other and I felt so out of place. I thought I was cool in my cut-off jeans, long hair and pale skinny body. But I was nothing compared to those Adonises. Some of them never even went in the water which I thought was kind of strange. All they wanted to do was flirt, pose, sunbathe and dance. And after that visit to Manhattan Beach, so did I.

That was the day that I told my mother and Walter that I wanted to start working out. They surprised me with a steel bench and a set of starter weights. I didn't know where to begin so I decided to do some research at the nearby library. With that knowledge and a bit of coaching from a neighbor, I put together my very own work-out routine. Everyday after work I went straight home and hit the weights for an hour and a half. For the first few months there was no change. It was a slow grueling process and there were days I felt like giving up. But once I started to see results, it motivated me even more. There was no doubt in my mind that by next summer I would be ready for Manhattan Beach.

My girlfriend Joanna wasn't crazy about my friend Ronnie. She was becoming more possessive and she had a mean jealous streak that I never seen before. She even went so far as to fix her girlfriend up with him just so she could be around us all the time.

The following spring I met Bob and Danny while smoking a joint at my favorite spot on Ocean Parkway and Avenue C. They were a really cool gay couple who owned an Afghan hound and lived in a luxury apartment building on that same corner. One day while they were smoking with me it started to rain. They invited me in to see their apartment and to listen to some music. I fell in love with their place from the moment I walked through the door. It was a modern one-bedroom apartment with shiny wooden floors. They had a huge portrait of the New York City skyline painted right on the wall above an enormous couch. Their stereo system was hidden in the closet along with hundreds of albums. I could tell they were proud of that place and very comfortable with their lifestyle.

The more I hung out there the more intrigued I became with them, their friends, and their music. I was always an open-minded person and never saw "different people" or "alternate lifestyles" as a threat. In a few weeks I came to realize that they weren't the only gay men living in that building. One night they all decided to take me out dancing to a club called 12 West. I was excited and nervous about it, but still curious enough to go.

It was located in Manhattan underneath the West Side Highway on the corner of West 12th Street. I never went dancing in my life and there I was standing on line in front of one of the most popular gay clubs in town. All the guys were wearing t-shirts, jeans, and sneakers. Some even walked around with no shirts on. It was extremely "cruisey" in there, but my friends were very protective of me. They sensed that I was uncomfortable so they sat with me for a while. Once I warmed up to the place, they left me alone to do my own cruising and then they went off to dance.

The sound system at that place was phenomenal. Needless to say, it was all disco music and Donna Summer ruled. You could tell that they loved her because whenever her songs came on everyone made a dash for the dance floor. Then they all would begin cheering and stomping their feet. After an hour, I finally got up the courage to go look for my friends who knew I would eventually join them. Once I stepped out on to that dance floor I was hooked. It crossed my mind, just like it did that day at Manhattan Beach, that I had found a new life.

At the top of the summer I put in an application for school. Ronnie was a student at St. Francis College and already in his second year. He convinced me to register, even though I had my heart set on going to HB Studio in Manhattan to study acting and voice. I thought it would cool to go to the same school as my friend. When I met him there to fill out the paperwork I told him to bring me to the financial aid office. He looked at me puzzled and said, "Financial aid office...why the hell are you applying for financial aid when your father's Pat Cooper?"

"I have to Ronnie...he won't pay for it."
"But he's so rich...he's famous...and he's your father."
"I know, Ronnie, I know...but he's impossible, and you don't know the whole story."

He could see that I was ashamed and from that day on he never brought up my father again. Everything worked out and the people in the financial aid office told me that I was eligible for some money. Two weeks before class I changed my mind and decided not to go to college.

In late August, I found out that my father was doing a few shows at the Walker movie theatre in Bensonhurst, Brooklyn. It was a predominantly Italian neighborhood and not too far from my house. It was the perfect opportunity for me to go see him, and take Joanna and my grandmother with me. I knew Joanna's parents would allow her to go this time because he was playing right in the neighborhood. My grandmother was another story because their relationship was strained and had been for years at this point. If there was anybody that I really wanted to take—it was her. I hadn't seen them in the same room together since the time she took me to the Copa when I was a little boy. It was my chance to return the favor. Maybe by me bringing her down there and with some help from God, my father would make up with her this time.

I bought three tickets a week in advance for his Saturday night performance. When I called my grandmother and told her that I was taking her to see her son, she tried talking her way out of it. She sounded uninterested and explained that the place would be too mobbed. After a little begging and explaining to her that I already bought the tickets, she gave in. I knew she wouldn't disappoint me or have me waste my money.

I borrowed my mother's car and picked up my grandmother first, then Joanna. They both looked terrific and knew each other from my past birthday party. When we got there, grandma was right—it was a mad house. My father knew we were coming and we wanted to try and find him, but it was too late. The show was about to begin and we had to take our seats. It was a full house and it looked like everybody in the place was Italian. There were some people standing along the back wall and in the balcony just to see him. They knew my father was born and raised in Brooklyn, and they were ready for him.

When he walked out on the stage the place went nuts. They were cheering so loudly that my grandmother looked at me like her eardrums were going to explode. Joanna was all excited and kept squeezing my leg every time the crowd went crazy. He must have been talking for about an hour and a half straight. They wouldn't let him get off that stage. Every time he said, "Good night," they screamed, "More."

When we got out in the lobby I heard people making comments about the show. Some were mimicking him; others were talking about buying more tickets for another night. My grandmother and Joanna were waiting on line to get into the bathroom and I was standing in the front looking around for my father. When the crowd finally cleared out my father appeared. We talked for about twenty minutes, but kept being interrupted by some of the fans that were still standing in front of the place. People kept coming in asking for autographs, and then when they saw my grandmother they wanted hers, too. Then out of nowhere my girlfriend makes a comment to my father about paying for our wedding. I thought my grandmother was going to stab her. I tried to play it off like she was kidding, but it was too late because my father already answered her. He told my girlfriend that he would pay her not to marry me. My grandmother looked at me and rolled her eyes.

After we said our goodbyes my father hopped in a limo and he was gone. We walked to the car in silence and my grandmother remained that way for most of the ride home. I was boiling and couldn't wait to drop my grandmother off so I could give Joanna a piece of my mind.

"Are you crazy, Joanna?"
"I was only kidding."

"You might have been kidding, Joanna, but my father doesn't know you and he doesn't know that. He thinks everybody is after his money, and what you said tonight only confirms his beliefs. Even my grandmother told me not to ask him for anything...and I'm his son. But by you asking him for that....to pay for our wedding...he'll think I put you up to it," I said.

"I'm sorry."
"I accept your apology but it's too late, Joanna. Did you see the look on my grandmother's face? You think I'm kidding. We

were so embarrassed and you made it worse for us." I let out a big sigh and realized I was wasting my breath trying to explain it to her. There was no way she would understand.

After I got home I knew it was too late to call my grand-mother. I let it go until the next day and then we had a big discussion about it. Needless to say, she wasn't too fond of Joanna and I'm sure my father wasn't either.

A few weeks went by and it was the end of the summer. It was also the end of Joanna and me. We broke up at Coney Island in the same spot where I used to go with my family. That morning she had a big fight with her parents and I knew what that meant; she'd be in a bad mood all day and take it out on me. What really got me going was when she said that she didn't want me to go dancing anymore. Then in the same breath she tells me that she wants to get engaged. I wasn't ready to get married, now or any time soon. And I told her that. I saw what happened to my mother and father, and some of my cousins. Even my grandmother and grandfather were divorced. That was not going to be my movie, too. I knew the real reason why she was pressuring me; she wanted to get out of her house and away from her parents. But that was no reason to get married, and I knew that even back then. She didn't appreciate my honesty and in the middle of the argument she scratched my arm. She purposely took her nails and dug them into my skin. That's when I grabbed my things and left the beach. I could hear her screaming my name, over and over again, but I never looked back.

My life was changing rapidly. My self-esteem was at an all time high and so was my testosterone. I was living at Manhattan Beach by day and partying in the clubs by night. If I couldn't get anyone to go to the beach with me, then I'd go alone, even if that meant taking the train or the bus. It was the same thing for the discos. I learned to enjoy dancing in all kinds of places with all kinds of people: straight, gay, and bisexual. Some of those people ended up being my close and dearest friends. Some even turned out to be my lovers.

Most of the clubs I went to were wild. It wasn't out of the or-
dinary to see people getting high or having sex in them. I was going
to a variety of clubs about two or three times a week. My mother
didn't like me taking the trains late at night, so when she knew that
I was going to the city she let me take her car. She always worried
either way and still waited up for me until I arrived home.

One night when I was leaving to go out my mother was walking the dog. As I passed by her she waved goodbye and said
something to me. Usually I would've just waved back at her and
kept on going. But that night I put the car in reverse, and went all
the way back to see what she wanted. I rolled down the window
and she told me to be careful. "Ma, you made me come back for
that. I'm late...I still have to pick up my friend...don't worry; I'm a
very good driver. I took Drivers Ed, remember?" Then before I
could reassure her some more the dog pulled her down the block.

That night I was going to Galaxy 21 a multi-level discotheque
located on West 23rd Street, in Manhattan. It wasn't my first
choice that night, and the only reason that I went there was because of my friend. It had two huge dance floors, one in the basement and the other one on the first floor by the bar. On the second
floor there was a large empty room where people went to make
out and fool around. It was completely dark in there, and the only
light was a small red bulb hanging from the ceiling in the center of
the room.

As soon as we walked in my friend Sal ran into some people that he knew. We all started talking and went over to the bar
for a drink. After twenty minutes of that I was bored and decided
to go for a walk. I kept thinking about that room upstairs and could-
n't wait to check it out. Once I stepped inside it took a few minutes
for my eyes to focus. I remember walking around with my arms
out in front of me just so that I wouldn't crash into anyone. When
my vision returned, I realized there wasn't much going on. I sat on
a make-shift platform watching a few people in the corner of the
room and listening to the blasting music from the floor below. I noticed another guy sitting to the right of me about ten feet away

doing the same thing. When I heard my favorite song come on, I jumped up and proceeded to leave the room. On the way out something hit me in the face. It felt like somebody walked into me and I didn't think anything of it. It wasn't until I got halfway down the stairs that I realized I was hurt. My initials on the left side of my skin-tight beige shirt were covered with blood. A few steps ahead of me was that same guy that I was sitting next to upstairs in the room. His guilty face kept looking back at me as he hurried out of the club. When I got to the bottom of the landing he was gone.

Feeling dazed and confused I approached a man who worked there and pointed to my mouth. Judging by the look on his face it didn't seem so bad. But when he told that I had a couple of teeth missing that's when I got scared. Everyone started gathering around and staring at me. I wanted to run into the bathroom and look at myself in the mirror, but he wouldn't let me. Instead, he said he was taking me to the hospital. Then from out of nowhere my friend appeared. The next thing I knew I was icing my lip and we were all in a cab heading downtown to St. Vincent's hospital.

Sal and I rushed in and they took me right away. The nurse immediately gave me a tetanus shot and told me that I needed stitches. She left me alone for about fifteen minutes before returning with the doctor. I sat there feeling depressed and wondering why this happened. What kind of person would do something like this to me, especially for no reason? I began thinking about my mother and all the years that we spent in the orthodontist's office just trying to straighten my teeth. Now, in a split second the front ones were gone; all because of some violent closet case who decided to hurt somebody that night. A couple of inches higher he would have blinded me for life.

When the nurse and doctor entered the room they gave me another needle. That one sent me through the roof. After numbing my lip they made me lie on the table where they proceeded to stitch me up. In ten minutes he was done and part one of my nightmare was over. Now I had to go home and break the news to my mother.

We hailed a cab and went back to pick up the car. The first thing I did after I got in was look in the rear view mirror at the damage done to my face. I analyzed myself like a forensic scientist while my friend Sal consoled me. I still had to drop him off and he lived about five miles away from me. He didn't want me to drive him all the way home and insisted on taking a cab the rest of the way. But I couldn't let him do that knowing that he stood with me in my darkest hour. I knew Sal for only three weeks and he already proved his friendship.

It was early morning now and beginning to get light out. My hand wouldn't stop shaking as I put the key into the front door. When I entered the dog greeted me in her usual fashion and then started licking the dried blood off of my shirt. When I walked into the living room my mother was sound asleep on the couch. There was nobody home that weekend except my sister. Walter had gone hunting with his son and they wouldn't be back for another day. I gently tapped my mother on the shoulder. As soon as she opened her eyes she let out a scream so loud that my sister came running down the stairs. My mother began sobbing uncontrollably and pacing around the room with a nervous energy that almost made her collapse.

On Monday morning we went to find out what had to be done with my teeth. My mother brought me to the oral surgeon first, where part two of my nightmare began. He had to take x-rays of my entire mouth and remove fragments of broken teeth still left under my upper gums. For a week I was in pain. I had to eat and drink through a straw, and then return back to his office to get my stitches taken out. When everything finally healed, I went to my regular dentist which meant another eight weeks of needles and more pain. In the end he replaced my missing teeth with a permanent bridge that consisted of six porcelain crowns.

During that period of restoration I was miserable and depressed. My holidays were ruined, I quit my job, and the only time I left the house was when I went to see the doctor. Even my throat was bothering me, and I knew I had to go back to the specialist and take care of that again. He wanted me to start working with a speech therapist as soon as I finished with my teeth. By then it was a year since I quit smoking cigarettes, and six months that I had stopped smoking pot. I did everything possible to make those little growths disappear and now he tells me that I needed to do more.

It took me almost two years to get my self-esteem to a good place and now after the accident it was at an all time low. I was afraid to go out dancing and angry at myself for not running after that guy in the club. The nightmare wouldn't go away and I had to relive it every time a concerned relative or friend called to ask what happened. All I wanted to do was put my life back together like the way it was before the accident. The only thing that kept me sane during that painful time in my life was working out, and I almost gave that up, too.

My father called the house about three weeks after I got hurt. It was a brief conversation and right to the point. As soon as I answered the house phone I heard my name.

"Mike,"

"Yeah,"

"It's your father...what happened that I'm getting all these bills from the dentist?"

"Hi Dad...I got hurt,"

"What do you mean you got hurt, and what are you doin hanging out in clubs like that, anyway?"

"What do you mean in clubs like that? All the clubs in the city are like that, Dad,"

"No they're not...I took a trip down there the other night and spoke with one of the owners. I know what goes on there, Mike."

"What goes on there? Nothing goes on there Dad."

"Never mind...so you decide to go to those kinds of places and now your father has got to pay for it."

"What do you mean, Dad? It's not my fault."

"No, but now I got to pay for it. Am I right? Let me ask you something. Suppose I didn't have the money to pay for your dentist bills? Then what would you do?"

"I don't know, Dad."

"You'd have to gum your food, Mike...that's what you'd do," he said.

"What...what do you mean? It's not my fault!" I screamed.

"Stay out of those clubs because next time I'm not paying for a god damn thing!" He yelled, and then slammed the phone down in my ear.

After that call I was devastated. I felt like I got punched in the face all over again. Throughout the whole conversation he never even asked me how I was feeling. I remembered the speech he gave to me about calling his house and speaking the correct way over the telephone. Here it was, less than a month after that hor-rific accident at the club where I could have been killed, and all he was worried about were the doctor bills he had to pay.

Chapter Seven
- Coming Out of the Dark -

It became painfully apparent to me that after my last conversation with my father I had to get on with my life without him. I would have to abandon the idea, for my own sanity and well being, of ever having a normal father and son relationship with him. I had gotten the message—loud and clear!

I celebrated my twenty first birthday and with it came great news. Bank of Boston hired me full time in their financial exchange department. My father didn't have to pay for my doctor bills now that I was twenty-one, so the timing couldn't have been better. I must admit that in some strange way, I felt relieved knowing that I didn't have to rely on him anymore for any form of financial support.

I had a few other dreams that I wanted to pursue and one of them was to become an actor. But before signing up for any classes I took my doctor's advice and went to see the speech therapist that he recommended months ago. He said she was a miracle worker and that it was imperative I see her before doing any form of vocalizing. After working with her for almost two months my polyps disappeared. When I returned to the doctor he gave me the green light and told me I could take as many classes as I wanted. Halleluiah! Now I could focus on making my dreams come true and become independent. I was in a good place again, and ready to start looking for my own apartment.

Getting my own place was another dream of mine that had been put on hold because of the accident. I started asking around the neighborhood and found out a woman up the block was looking to rent out the attic in her house. She gave me a great deal and made it affordable. I believe that place fell into my lap totally because of fate. It was meant to be. At that time my mother and Walter were thinking of moving to Long Island and they wanted me to go with them. But I had already made up my mind that I didn't want to leave Brooklyn.

The whole experience of being on my own thrilled me. My bachelor apartment was phenomenal; it had two bedrooms and a private entrance. The apartment was completely furnished by my mother and grandmother. My grandmother gave me a huge couch for the living room and a cot for the extra bedroom. My mom gave me her old bedroom set and utensils for the kitchen. In less than a month they both had turned that attic apartment into a palace.

It was very convenient living on the same block as my mother. For the first few months I was eating there almost every night. On the weekends she did my laundry and let me borrow her car. Even my grandmother worried about me. When I went to visit her, besides feeding me to death, she'd send me home with tons of cooked food in plastic containers to hold me over. I had it made and never had to worry about cooking or anything else. I knew sooner or later I would have to learn how to cook for myself.

Well when that day came my grandmother was more than eager to teach me. The first thing I wanted to know was how to make her sauce. I soon realized it was a lot of work and very time consuming. She had a great deal of patience doing all that work every week. The part that I had the most difficulty with was making the meatballs. I fried more than a dozen of those babies and placed them carefully into the sauce. When I took them out of the pot they were hard as rocks. The following week I tried again, but this time I called my grandmother and had her walk me through all the steps again. I never got an award for that class, but I did learn how to make a damn good sauce and a tasty meatball.

That year everybody that I was close to was either extremely busy with their lives or had moved away. Even the gay guys that lived around the corner from me had moved. It was time to make a concerted effort to get out more, check out the club scene around Brooklyn, and make some new friends.

One night when I was at a club I met a guy named Chris. He lived in Bensonhurst and worked for the airlines. He mostly flew international flights and liked to tell me all about his adventures. I was so impressed that he was only five years older than me and already had seen half the world. We became like brothers and started hanging out as much as we could. One day, out of the blue, he asked me to be his roommate. It was perfect timing again because my mother had just moved to Long Island. She had been like a safety net for the past year and now there was no reason for me to stay on the block.

I celebrated New Year's Eve in my new huge two-bedroom apartment, located on the second floor in a private house. I was so excited about moving into the Bensonhurst section of Brooklyn. Bensonhurst was right smack in the middle of everything and it had the best restaurants, bakeries, gyms, and clubs.

The apartment was a score, but too big and needed a lot of work. I didn't have the money, time, or the enthusiasm to tackle it. Fortunately, Chris did. He made a deal with the landlord and she got someone to paint the whole place for us. That was half the battle. Now we had seven rooms, seventeen windows, a huge walk-in-closet, and a back porch to contend with. Just putting shades and curtains on all those windows was enough to bankrupt us. We went for months without anything in that apartment, except two beds and a couch. I left most of my old furniture behind out of pure laziness and now I had to start from scratch. There were no freebies or jumpstarts this time around.

Not long after moving in with Chris my mother gave me the biggest surprise of my life. She presented me with the keys to her car as a birthday gift. She even packed the back seat with sentimental things, including a couple of my plants that I forgot to take when she moved. I was surprised by how much stuff she saved and that she still had those plants. One was a gigantic gardenia bush that I grew for her because she loved the smell of those flowers. In fact, when she married my father her wedding bouquet was loaded with them. The other was a marijuana plant that I told her was a baby mimosa tree. She had been taking care of them for the past year and placed the marijuana plant in front of the St. Jude statue because it wasn't doing so well. I am forever grateful to him that she never caught on or else it would have been my last birthday. At least I was smart enough to tell her it was mimosa instead of basil; otherwise she would have thrown some of it in the sauce and then she really would have killed me when she found out it was pot.

My life was going really well. I started to seriously pursue my acting career. Some of the best classes and the majority of the auditions were held during the day. Having a nine to five office job wasn't cutting it anymore. I needed something more flexible and that's when I began my short career in the restaurant industry.

My first job was a busboy and it turned out to be a disaster. After three long weeks working at a small restaurant in Greenwich Village they let me go. I was disappointed, but I had what I needed to talk my way into a bigger and better place.

Next stop was the River Café. I knew from the moment I stepped onto that cobble-stoned driveway that I wanted to work there. It is an elegant waterfront restaurant sitting in the East River underneath the Brooklyn Bridge. The candle-lit dining room is all windows, the atmosphere is romantic, and the view of downtown Manhattan is breathtaking. I enjoyed working there for a while and once I got some more experience I decided to move on.

My last position in the restaurant business was across the river at Windows on the World. This famous landmark restaurant was located on top of the north tower in the World Trade Center and had a spectacular panoramic view of the city. It was a cool place to work and just as beautiful as the River Café except that I wasn't making enough money there. I didn't know what to do or where to look next.

One morning I got to work a little earlier than usual and noticed some guy fussing with all the flowers and plants. Watching him brought back memories of when I was a kid and used to work for a flower shop. Windows had the most magnificent floral arrangements I had ever seen, and I was curious to find out which florist he was from. He told me that he worked at the store located in the main concourse level of the building. I asked him if they needed any help and he told me to speak to a woman named Barbara who was one of the owners. As soon as I finished work I hopped into the express elevator and flew down to the store.

When I first entered the Garden Path I was surprised to see how many people worked there. Everyone was busy doing something and Barbara was in the back showing the guys how to clean the roses. I told her that I was looking for a job and that I would love to work in a flower shop again. Once she heard that I had some experience, she hired me on the spot. It was just like that and she expected me to be there at nine the next morning.

I spent the first six months at The Garden Path cleaning the flowers and making deliveries. When we were slow I took the opportunity to watch the designers so I could learn how to make exotic arrangements and fancy bouquets. I even took a class at the Bronx Botanical Gardens to perfect my skills. I loved the creative side of the store and eventually became interested in the business aspect, too.

When the bosses found out that I used to be a bank teller they offered me a cashier's position. I jumped at the opportunity because it meant more money and shorter hours. They even gave me the convenience of a free parking space located in the basement of the building.

That job fit perfectly into my life and being the evening manager gave me the luxury of having my days free. The extra money allowed me to join a gym and register for a couple of more classes at my acting school.

Not long after starting at the Garden path my father unexpectedly came back into my life. I met with him for the first time in four years and nothing changed except the restaurant. We started meeting for lunch downtown in Little Italy, instead of in midtown like we used to. It was apparent now more than ever that these little "get-togethers" every couple of years was going to be the extent of our relationship. By this time I knew I was never going to be invited out to his house in Las Vegas. I was never going to swim in his pool or even drive any of his luxurious cars. He was never going to come over my house for dinner, or even stop by to see what it looked like. I was no longer frustrated with that reality and finally accepted the fact that it wasn't ever going to get better. It was what it was!

It was during this time that I noticed my father had become very bitter. He seemed mad at the world and started bad-mouthing everyone, including our family. It used to make me sick hearing him say such terrible things about the people I loved. It was bad enough that we never really talked. Now I had to sit there and listen to crap like this coming out of his mouth. He would speak to me like he wasn't part of the same family. Yet he wanted to know who, what, when and why. It got crazy sometimes and I felt like I was being interrogated. I used to always ask him the same question: "What does all this have to do with me, Dad?" And his disturbing response never changed. "You come from the same crop. I know you Mike...you play both sides down the middle, and your fathers no fool. You're one of those people!" And while he was talking and busy putting me down, I'd be having another conversation in my head that went like this: "What the hell are you talking about, Dad? You come from the same crop as me. And you're one of those people, too!" Sometimes I just felt like getting up and walking away from him. But something inside kept me there and I really believed that if I let him vent a few times, he would eventually stop. But he never did! His ranting and raving sounded like a new routine. All I ever wanted to do was enjoy his company and be a son. That was my only agenda. I don't understand why he couldn't see that.

My roommate Chris was having a terrible year. He lost both of his parents within six months of each other. First was his paralyzed mother who died from a stroke. Then, six months later his father passed away from a sudden heart attack. Chris was an only child and inherited the house. He was a landlord now and told me that he would be moving back home. I couldn't afford the apartment by myself and needed to find another roommate real fast.

I knew a guy named Bill that I thought would be interested. He lived in Astoria, Queens, and would end up becoming one of my all time closest friend. We met at a club called, "The Ice Palace," located on West 57th Street and 6th Avenue in Manhattan. At first we used to just speak on the telephone and meet at the club. But after he moved in with me we became real tight and cultivated a friendship that would last for many years. We did everything together and shared many common interests. I could always count on Bill to be there for me.

The day after Bill moved in was my mother's forty-ninth birthday. I headed over to her house to celebrate and to help my stepfather replace my car speakers. He had promised to do that for me if I gave him a few pointers about working out. He had been diagnosed with prostate cancer a year earlier and felt that some exercising would do him good.

My stepfather was a man of rare talent. I watched him spend ten years of his life fixing and rebuilding things for the house just to please my mother. He was totally altruistic and enjoyed doing things for others. He did things for everybody, including my grandmother, and he respected her more than my own father ever did.

I remember he treated me extra special that day. As soon as we finished eating, he started working on my car while my sister snuck away to get my mother's birthday cake. He spent almost an hour outside in the cold fiddling with all the wires, and I could tell he was tired. When he was through we had dessert, and then I was on my way. After pulling out of the driveway, I realized that I forgot to show him the exercises. I felt bad, and then remembered I would be seeing him again the following week on Easter Sunday when we would be able to go over a few things. I took off down the block and as soon as I turned the corner I blasted my new speakers.

When I called them on Tuesday morning I got no answer. I tried them again an hour later and there was still no answer, so I decided to get ready for work. I was about to jump into the shower when the phone rang. It was my sister and she was crying hysterically. I could hardly make out what she was saying until I heard the words, "Walter's dead!" Suddenly it felt like all time had stopped. She told me that my mother was still at the hospital and that they were going to do an autopsy on him. The next thing I knew I was in the car with my sister driving out to my mother's house.

When I think about my mother and some of the curve balls that have been thrown at her, it breaks my heart. In 1960 it was the break-up of her marriage to my father. Then to make matters worse she lost her mother a few years after that. It wasn't until she met Walter that her life began to change for the better. She got married, moved a few times, and finished raising my sister and I. Walter found the house of their dreams; they settled in, and were finally looking at peace and contentment for the rest of their lives. They were living there for only two years before she suffered the misfortune of losing a wonderful man that loved and protected her.

For the remainder of the year my sister and I did the best we could to try to help my mother get back on her feet. I went out there as much as possible to comfort her, and my sister decided to move back home. Eventually my mother got a job and began to move on with her life. Working kept her mind occupied and for that alone it was a blessing.

One year after my friend Bill moved in with me he told me that he was looking to move out. He applied for a one-bedroom apartment a few blocks away in a luxury building and suggested that I move in with him. It was the best decision I ever made and

one of my most carefree summers. He didn't charge me anything
to live there and that gave me the chance to save up for the security and the one-month's rent that I would need for my own apartment in the same building. Finally in six months, I got my own place
on the ninth floor facing the front of the building.

I moved into apartment 9L, which was the best apartment
I ever had and the most luxurious. On a clear night I could see the
parachute ride and the Ferris wheel at Coney Island from my ter-
race. They looked beautiful, especially on the fourth of July with
the spectacular fireworks display in the background. I still had
my old bedroom set and the television that my mother gave me.
My grandmother donated her wicker chairs to hold me until I
could afford to buy a couch for the living room. I even had a doorman in the lobby to take my packages and greet my guests. The
best part about living in that building was that my friends lived
there, too. I enjoyed their company and did everything with them.
If I wasn't downstairs eating with Bill, then I was upstairs watching television with Bob. There was never a dull moment—and if
we got bored, we'd go visit somebody else in the building or take
a ride in the car. We became like family!

The Garden Path was a lucrative business and they were always looking for honest help. In addition to the store, my bosses
owned flower stands throughout the lobby of the building where
they sold small inexpensive bouquets. The concourse area of the
World Trade Center was extremely busy. That's when Bill and my
cousin come into the picture. On my recommendation, my
bosses hired the both of them. We had loads of fun working together.

My grandmother loved stopping by the store. She came by
quite often and always with one of her sisters. My boss told me
to give her anything she wanted. Whenever she came in I would
pack up a dozen long stem American Beauty red roses for her.
Then she would make me put them back and tell me she preferred the miniature carnations instead.

I would look at her like she was crazy and say, "Are you kidding me? I want to give you the best flowers in the store, grandma. You want this crap instead?"

"Why not... I like them better...they last longer. Just make sure you throw in a good vase for me," she said.

I would laugh and say, "Okay gram...whatever you want."

My bosses got a kick out of her and they knew that she was Pat Cooper's mother. When I first started working there I had told them who my father was. Now four years later and after meeting my grandmother, they wanted to meet her son. They asked me if I could get him to do a show across the hall at the Market Bar and Restaurant. At first I thought they were kidding and I just shrugged it off. But when Barbara told me that they spoke with the restaurant owners already, then I knew they were serious. It was time to tell them the situation with my father and the kind of relationship we had. I confided in Barbara because she was my favorite boss and the one who hired me. When she heard the story she was quite surprised, but wanted me to ask him anyway. I promised her that I would call him as soon as he came back to New York.

At that time it was easy to get in touch with my father. He had an apartment in Greenwich Village that he used when he was in town. I had his phone number and he had an answering machine. The days of hunting him down and calling hotels were over. He told me that he felt safer in an apartment because he had a frightening experience in one of the hotels. Someone put something underneath his door that knocked him out for almost twenty-four hours. Then they broke in and robbed him. That was the first scare of his life and I kinda felt sorry for him. But I wasn't at all sympathetic when I heard the second one. He told me that he recently had a small growth removed from his throat. It turned out to be benign, but I could tell he was still shaken up a bit about it, anyways. I looked at him and with my head cocked to one side I said, "I had the same exact thing, Dad, remember? Except that I didn't need to have it removed like yours" But what I really wanted to say to him was: "You didn't look that worried when I told you that I had polyps in my throat. The only thing you were worried about was the bills; remember Dad? You didn't even believe me." I don't know what he was looking for or expected me to say to him that day, but he damn sure wasn't getting any sympathy out of me.

I kept my promise to Barbara and called my father. I popped the question and to my surprise he agreed to meet with my bosses. They made a deal on Monday and he was all set to perform at The Market Bar and Restaurant on Friday.

The night of his performance I had to work. I didn't mind because I could still hear his voice from where I was standing inside the store. As a matter of fact, my friend Bill could hear him better than me because the flower stand was closer to the restaurant. A couple of times he took care of the customers for me so that I could run across the hall and see what was happening. It was so crowded in there that I couldn't even get past the bar to see my father. Later, while I was busy counting out the register my father walked in. He handed me some cash and told me to count it. It was five hundred dollars.

"What's this for?" I asked.

"It's for you. You got me the job and you get ten percent, just like my agent would have gotten."

"Wow! Thanks Dad. Thanks a lot! I'm leaving in five minutes. Wait for me, Okay. I want you to come see my apartment," I said.

"I can't Mike, I'm..."

I interrupted him and said, "C'mon Dad. It'll only take a half an hour...then I'll drive you back to the city. It's a beautiful apartment...it's like the one you used to have on West End Avenue."

"Mike, what's there to see in an apartment? All apartments are alike."

"But Dad this is different...it's the best place I ever had," I explained.

"Not tonight, Mike...I'm tired, I just got done working."

"All right, whatever you say...maybe next time. You need a lift?" I asked.

"No, I'm just gonna catch a cab in front of the hotel and I'll be home in five minutes. Take care, be good...I'll call ya," he said as he walked out of the store.

On the way home I poured my heart out to Bill. I told him that I would have preferred it if my father had given me ten percent of his time rather than ten percent of what he earned. All I ever wanted from him was some attention and to hear him say, just once, that he was proud of me. That's why I tried to convince him to come back to my place. I knew he would have been impressed and maybe have said it then. But as usual, he never seemed interested in any aspect of my life. Even when I told him that I was going to acting school or that I was a manager in a flower shop, he knocked me down. He was extremely critical and told me that acting schools were a waste of time. He bragged that he never went to school for show business and that the only thing I would become was a professional student for the rest of my life. He even belittled my job at the store. He said the only reason to be working in a flower shop is if I had plans to open up my own place someday. I could never win with my father and never understood why it was so difficult for him just to say something positive to me.

When I returned to work on Monday I was sure the topic of conversation was going to be about my father and the show. Instead, everyone was talking about Barbara's health. She was diagnosed with cancer and we were shocked. It was a rough year for her and she spent most of the time out of the store. She traveled to Europe a couple of times seeking alternative treatment, but it was no use. In less than a year she was gone. Barbara was the backbone of The Garden Path and after she passed away things started to get ugly around there. I knew I had to become more aggressive about pursuing my acting career or I was never going to get out of that place.

About a week after the show some unexpected visitors came down to the store. They were my father's friends and they knew I worked there. When they came in they introduced themselves and I thought they were there to buy some flowers. But in ten minutes I realized that they had stopped by for another reason. One of the women started talking to me about my father and his relationship with me. She caught me off guard and I felt that she was prying, but I engaged in the conversation anyway. From what she was saying, I could tell that my father told her some private things about us. I wanted to tell her my side of the story and set the record straight. When we were through talking the last thing she said was: "He's still your father and no matter what, you should respect him." I was insulted by her comment and before she left I made sure she knew that I never disrespected my father. I also made sure that all three of them knew it was the other way around; that my father was the one who had a respect problem, even with his own mother.

The following night he called me at the flower shop. I had a feeling I'd hear from him, but I didn't think so soon. In seconds, we were in the middle of a heavy conversation.

"Mike, what did you say to those people last night?" He asked.

"Dad, what do you mean what did I say to those people? Wait...Dad, Hold on...let me take the other phone in the back," I said.

I ran outside to the front and motioned to Bill to watch the store. Then I went in the office and picked up the phone. I knew this could take awhile.

"Dad"

"Mike...I know you're at work...so I'll be brief. What are you doin discussing my business with these people?"

"Discussing your business...what do you mean? They're the ones that came down to the store, dad."

"I already spoke with them and told them they were out of line. But, you still don't have to tell people your business, Mike."

"Dad...it was obvious that they knew things. I didn't tell them any of that stuff. How did they know where I even worked? They're your friends and they were very nice people. So, I tried to be as polite as I could...but they were prying. What did you want me to do, throw them out of the store... or be rude to them?" I asked.

"No, Mike...no...they had no right to do that. They won't be down there to bother you anymore. They're friends of mine, but I still told them that they stepped out of line by putting their nose in my business. I was annoyed at them and they knew they were wrong. I just finished speaking to them."

"Sure, Dad...no problem."

"I took care of it. Okay...let me let you go. It sounds like you're getting busy over there."

"I am...a few more customers just walked in. I'm gonna have to go, Dad."

"Okay, Mike...I'll talk to you. Be good...bye."

When I got off the phone I didn't have time to really think about anything. It wasn't until I got in the car and was on my way home that I began to vent. My poor friend Bill had to sit there and listen to it, again. The most disturbing part of the whole situation was that I had proof that my father was talking about personal family matters with other people. It was upsetting enough that he was bad mouthing the family to me, now he was going around saying God knows what to everybody else. He never thought it would backfire on him; nevertheless he was trying to cover his tracks by putting the blame on me. I believe that his friends had good intentions and thought maybe they could fix things, but it was clear to me that my father's objective wasn't the same.

That summer I spent most of my weekends at the beach. When I was with my friends the beach of choice was usually Riis Park. When I was with my grandmother there was no choice, it was always Coney Island. One day I convinced her to break her routine and go with me to Riis Park. She had no idea that I intended to take her to the nude section; in fact, she didn't even know that place existed. I couldn't wait to see the expression on her face and turn her on to a new experience.

When I arrived at her house she was already waiting outside for me. She was standing there with her beach chairs and her sister-in-law, Bina. Aunt Bina was married to my grandfather's brother who passed away at a young age and left her with five kids. The thing I remember most about Aunt Bina was that she didn't speak English. My grandmother knew enough Italian to have a conver-

126

sation with her, but I didn't understand a word of it. Aunt Bina communicated with me through hand movements and facial expressions. An animated conversation I used to call it. Then the rest we depended on my grandmother. I didn't expect her to be there that day and I wasn't opposed to her going with us; however, I was a little bit worried what her children were going to say when they found out where I took her. My intentions were to play a joke on my grandmother. I knew she could handle it, but Aunt Bina, I wasn't too sure about. Nevertheless, I took her along and figured we'd all have a few good laughs.

It took us more than forty-five minutes to get there because of all the traffic. The parking lot was packed which meant that the beach would be, too. As soon as we got out of the car she rolled her eyes and handed me her aluminum chairs. She grabbed her straw bag from the back seat, which was filled with tons of stuff, and then hurried us towards the beach. When we stepped onto the sand she let out a huge sigh and said,

"Finally...now let's see what's so special about this place."
"Gram...this is not it. It's much further down. Let's walk along the shore...it'll be easier for you," I said.
"Where the hell are you taking us? What's wrong with right here?" She said.
"This is not the place I want to show you. We have to walk down a couple of more bays to get there," I said.
"You got a head like a brick...ugh! Alright, lead the way mister," she said.

She looked at Bina and said something in Italian. Aunt Bina nodded her head and said something back. They got into a conversation and continued to follow me.

"One more bay...one more bay," I shouted as I waited for them to catch up. My grandmother raised her fist in the air. She looked aggravated and I knew that I made a mistake bringing them there. But, it was too late and now I had to make the best of it.

I plopped the chairs down on the outskirts of Bay 1. It would be close enough for them to see everything without putting them in the middle of it all. It didn't take my grandmother five minutes to realize what was going on.

"This is what you brought me all the way here for. You gotta have your head examined...you really do," she said.

I laughed and decided to sit with them for a while to make sure they were okay. There was an old man standing a short distance in front of us. He was completely naked except for a baseball cap. When Aunt Bina saw him she became a bit uncomfortable and sat on the blanket covering both eyes with her hands. Every so often she separated her fingers and snuck a peek at the guy. Then she'd mumble something in Italian to my grandmother and by her reaction I kinda knew what she was saying. My grandmother was totally unbothered by the nudity and I was amazed how she just sat there taking in the sights. She sat quietly for about ten minutes drinking her coffee and then slowly turned to me and said,

"You think I never seen a dickey before...you forgot that I had five kids. Bina had five kids, too. Remember, I made you...you didn't make me. You know how unsanitary that is...with all that sand stuck to his thing. He'll get a good infection...and it'll fall off. You'll see...then maybe next time he'll learn to keep it covered."

I laughed so hard and never expected my grandmother to say something like that. When she repeated her thoughts to Aunt Bina, she started cracking up, too.

"You think I'm kidding. It's worse for the women. Believe what I'm telling you...believe what I'm telling you,"

My grandmother never forgot that day and I learned that she was smarter and much more open-minded than I thought. There were no issues with Aunt Bina or that side of the family, either. In fact, when my cousins found out they were hysterical, too.

I spent the rest of the year trying to go on as many auditions as I could. I must have sent a photo and resume out to every casting director in Manhattan. Then I would follow up with a telephone call or a postcard picture to remind them that I was still looking for work. I did everything I was supposed to do and all I ever got in return was a whole bunch of rejection. I even waited on long lines just to get a chance to read for someone and maybe get a break.

My family knew I was frustrated and encouraged me to find something else. They didn't want me to give up my dream; they just thought it would be wise to have a backup in case the whole show business idea didn't work out. I couldn't decide on what else I wanted to do. I just knew it had to be something creative and in the entertainment industry. After doing my homework and racking my brains for a month, I finally found a school which caught my interest. The Center for Media Arts had an intense program which consisted of sound engineering, radio announcing, and television broadcasting. I enjoyed the classes, but found myself leaning more towards television with aspirations of becoming a talk show host. It was exactly what I was looking for and believed it would eventually be my ticket out of the flower shop. I set my priorities straight. I concentrated on school, put the acting aside for a while, and spent valuable time with the family.

The club scene wasn't the same anymore, at least not for me. Disco was being replaced by house and other kinds of music that seemed foreign to me. My favorite clubs had perished and the crowd in the new ones seemed much younger. The Palladium was the only club I went to that year, and that was because of my friend Bill who turned me on to it.

On Mother's Day I decided to take my grandmother to the Palladium. I always wanted to do something different, something extra special that would be a first time experience for her. Taking her to the Palladium that night gave me the chance to show her how much I appreciated all the first time experiences that she gave me. Now it was my turn to show her off and bring her someplace that she would remember for the rest of her life.

I picked her up around 6:30 and she was raring to go. My spry grandmother was all dressed up for the occasion in her lavender pants suit, complimented by a multi-color flowery blouse and classic leather pumps. Her accessories included the usual cameo brooch and a pair of gold clip-on earrings. My grandmother's hair was all done up and perfect as always. She was dressed to kill!

On the way there I kept debating with myself whether or not I should tell her it was gay night. After the Riis Park experience, I didn't think there was anything else I could do that would shock my grandmother. Either way she'd have a good time and still be fascinated with the place. My grandmother was never judgmental and always up for some adventure. With that in mind, I decided to keep my mouth shut and let her figure it out for herself. I just couldn't wait to show her what I've been doing for the past ten years.

The Palladium was fairly crowded when we walked in and the first thing I did was give her the grand tour. We weren't even there for ten minutes and already she had a smile on her face. After familiarizing her with the place we went downstairs by the bar where we stood and observed the crowd for a while. We had a great view of the dance floor, but there was nobody dancing. My grandmother seemed puzzled by this and I explained to her that it would change in a matter of seconds once they started playing some of the more popular stuff. Finally, the deejay put on some of the oldies. When the classic, "It's Raining Men" (by the Weather Girls) came on, it felt like the room exploded. All of a sudden there was a mad rush to get on the dance floor. That's when I grabbed my grandmother's arm and steered us both into the eye of the storm. We ended up in the middle of the crowd, dancing and twirling around with our hands up in the air. The whole night was worth it just for that moment alone. I never thought she had it in her. We danced before at weddings and all, but not like this. Everybody was looking and trying to dance with her. They treated my grandmother like a celebrity and I could see that she was getting a kick out of all the attention.

Suddenly confetti and balloons were dropping from the ceiling. Grandma said it looked more like New Year's Eve than it did Mother's Day. Then they slowly lowered a make-believe house, which resembled the one in "The Wizard of Oz." The music stopped for a few seconds and was replaced by the screaming voice of the wicked witch. I forgot to tell her about the special affects and when she saw the house coming down she rushed off the dance floor. She thought it was intermission and later admitted to me that it was a bit overwhelming.

We were about to sit down when a tall good looking older man approached us. He was all dressed up in a tuxedo and introduced himself as Tom. He was friendly and somewhat flirtatious, too. We started talking and he thought it was really cool that I brought my grandmother to the club. He kept complimenting me and I had a funny feeling that he might ask me to dance. That was the last thing I wanted him to do in front of my grandmother. Besides, I didn't feel like dancing with anybody or meeting anyone. It was her night to shine, not mine. Then all of a sudden he turned to me and said, "Do you mind if I dance with your grandmother?" I was dumbfounded! I never expected that to come out of his mouth and to top it off he was asking for my permission. How the hell did my grandmother manage to get picked up by a straight man, her own age, on gay night at the Palladium? They danced to a Madonna song and then my grandmother politely said goodbye. Tom was a true gentleman. He thanked my grandmother, then came over and thanked me.

My grandmother and I spent the last half hour hanging out and talking in the balcony. She was tired and just wanted to rest her feet for a few minutes before heading home. The hit, "Girls Just Want to Have Fun" was playing, and I told her that we would be leaving right after that song. She was tapping her fingers to the music when out of the blue she said, "Where are all the girls at?" Suddenly at the end of the night she had a major revelation. "There aren't enough of them here, she said. Why do you think the men are dancing with each other? When I tell the girls where all the good-looking men are, then you won't have that problem here anymore. It's the best kept secret, this place." As I mentioned before, my grandmother knew me better than anyone!

I burst out laughing and took that as our cue to leave. On the way home the word "gay" never even came up. She spoke about all the fun she had and how she felt like a young girl again. I felt proud knowing that I gave her such a beautiful memory.

One of the things I treasured about my grandmother was the way she actively participated in my life. The talks, the dinners, and the surprises are just some of the things that mattered to me the most. It was the little things she did, like the time she gave me a picture of herself. For my birthday she always offered to take me downtown to buy me a brand new pair of sneakers and some clothes. That summer I asked her to go to a studio and take a professional photograph of herself to give to me for a birthday gift. I told her to have it framed so that I could hang it on my wall. Within days she handed me a beautifully wrapped five by seven colored picture of herself. She had it mounted and glossed on a fancy piece of wood. My grandmother even gave me the hooks to hang it up. She did all that and only because I had asked her to.

In the fall it was time for my final project at school and my grandmother agreed to let me interview her on videotape. The nineteen questions I had asked her were about her life and her estranged relationship with her son. Her responses were remarkably candid and similar to the many private conversations that we had over dinner.

I stopped by her house and pre-interviewed her a week prior to the actual taping. It went smoothly, and after the first couple of questions she even forgot that my tape recorder was on. By the time we were done she realized the emotional significance of my project. I wanted to make sure she was comfortable talking about my father, especially in front of the camera. The situation was extremely sensitive and the first time she would be speaking publicly about it. Of course I wanted to get a good grade, but not at the expense of hurting or embarrassing her. "A Mother's Story" was to be a portrait of her soul and a heart-rending testimony of the love she had for her son.

I met my grandmother at her house around eight in the morning. She was as perky as ever; all dressed up in a tangerine pants suit, and ready to go. One thing about her, she never kept me waiting. We took the train into the city and arrived at the school right on time. When we walked into the classroom, I introduced my grandmother to the instructor and then we both took our places on the stage waiting to begin. It was only in the last five minutes while looking over my notes that I started to get the jitters. When I glanced over at my grandmother, she unexpectedly gave me a big smile. She must have been watching me and somehow knew I needed that. I immediately felt at ease.

Suddenly the room went dark. There was complete silence, a few seconds of nothing, then the teacher's voice, "On five, four, three, two, and one." As soon as he signaled me with his hand, I started my introduction looking directly into the camera.

ME: Good morning, I'm Michael Caputo and my guest today is Louise Caputo. Louise Caputo is the mother of comedian Pat Cooper. She has been a mother for fifty-nine years and a grandmother for thirty-two years. She has dedicated her whole life to raising her family and her children. Her relationship with her son Pat Cooper is not what it seems because to hear Pat's act and albums one would get the impression that Pat is the closest dad and son to his family. Pat's whole act centers around his mother, his father, and his family. But the total opposite exists today. And with me today is Louise Caputo, to tell the story as it was and as it is today. (I look at my grandmother and begin the interview)

ME: So tell me Louise…how does it feel to be a mother and grandmother after all these years?

133

GRANDMA: Well, to me he's only a son. That's all I'm interested in. As long as he made money and he got on top where he wanted to be...I was very happy. So, to me it doesn't matter whether he changed his name...or he is Pat Caputo or Pat Cooper. He's still Pat Caputo. That's my name and that's what I brought him up with.

ME: How does it feel to be a mother and grandmother after all these years?

GRANDMA: Wonderful! Wonderful! I have a beautiful family. Everyone is talented. My grandchildren are more talented than my children. And all I ask for them is health and happiness. That's all that matters. All the money in the world can't take that place.

ME: Is it hard being Pat Cooper's mother?

GRANDMA: No, it isn't. I don't even tell anybody because I feel, well, they won't respect me as Louise Caputo. They would respect me as Pat Cooper's mother and that would be aggravating. I say...I like to be respected for myself. I have friends for sixty years, for forty years, and we always were interested in each other's dinners and each other's places. My grandchildren and everybody comes over for the holidays. It's still me, Louise Caputo...not Pat Cooper's mother. I'm still Louise Caputo. That's the way I brought him up...that everybody comes to the house and eats there. When Christmas Eve comes, it's open house for everybody. I love it and I'll always love it. Now that I'm getting a little older, I keep saying I don't want to do it anymore. But it always brings me back. I can't change for the world, but he has changed.

ME: How does it make you feel that seventy-five percent of his act is basically about his mother and his family?

GRANDMA: I know. I know. When he was growing up I was like an old bag...really a big old bag. I weighed two hundred fifty pounds. I had long hair and a big bun on my head. We weren't interested in clothes...you weren't interested in anything. All you were interested in was bringing them up. And they made fun of me. Every time they used to make fun of me because I used to go on Delancey Street and look for bargains...and dress up according to. I was always pregnant, that's something you couldn't help. Today, there are so many conveniences, but we never had conveniences. We just had kids, and food, and work. That was the whole thing in a life.

ME: Did you ever think that he would become so successful talking about his mother and his family?

GRANDMA: Oh yeah...yeah, because he always wanted to be a comedian and he's a great comedian. He could sing up a storm too, but he never cared to sing. All my children are talented. I have a daughter who's a great singer. I have another daughter who's an artist. I have grandchildren who are great actors and singers. I often wonder where all this talent came from. Was it the beans and lentils I gave them? (We both laugh)

ME: Has he always talked about becoming a comic?

GRANDMA: Always...always. Every time he joked around, his father would stop him. He loved it and till today he still loves it. But the idea is...he figures now he's big and there's no room in his life for his family. There is none. It doesn't bother me. As long as I know he's well and he's making it. That's all that matters. He's got his own family.

ME: Somewhere along the way he changed his name from Caputo to Cooper. Did that ever bother you?

GRANDMA: No...no...it never bothered me. It's just a name on a check. That's all changing your name is. But underneath you were born Pat Caputo and you can't take that away...because the roots are there. He'll never be different. He took after his father and that's the way he is. (She is self-assured and smiles at me)

ME: Has success changed him?

GRANDMA: It has! It has! But sooner or later he'll go back to Caputo because the roots are there and you can't change people's roots. (She smiles)

ME: Has success changed you? (I smile back at her as I ask the question)

GRANDMA: Nothing! Well, I lost weight. I started dying my hair after the kids got married. I had to do something for myself because I was tired of hearing the same thing—my mother this way, my mother that way. Now he can't believe it because everybody goes, "Oooh, that can't be your mother...that can't be your mother."

ME: Because you always had the bun and everything.

GRANDMA: Yeah, because I always had a bun. I never wore earrings. I never wore make-up. I was a redhead. He was a blond and my grandchildren were all redheads. But now they all changed, too. As he changed, we changed. But he can't accept the fact. Because when I do meet him and I'm all dressed up he goes, "Boy, what a change Ma, what a change." It really is a change.

ME: Do people treat you differently because you're his mother? When they find out do they say, there's Pat Cooper's mother, there's Pat Cooper's mother...looking for that bun?

GRANDMA: Yes...they do, they do. They don't believe it's possible that I was once like that. I tell them...when you have five kids, and all those sisters and brothers...believe me I was like that. You never—never thought clothes. Nobody ever did years ago, nobody in the world. It was continuous cooking, continuous having children. This one gave birth...that one gave birth, and that's all you did. So how could I be any different? The roots are there. You can't change those roots.

ME: Do you think that Pat let's people believe that he's a lot closer to his family and mother? (She interrupts the question and quickly responds)

GRANDMA: Oh yes, he does. He does. But he has to mingle with people that have money, society people, and a better class of people. I'm still used to eating with my hands. (She laughs) I'm still used to cooking and having all my grandchildren come over. We don't look at the special dinner table, special cut glass, special forks and knives. I've been to places where they gave me ten pieces of cutlery and nothing to eat. (We both laugh) That's ninety-nine percent of the stuff that goes on today. But we still cook. We still have a fork and a knife. I can't change. I just can't change.

ME: If you had to change anything about the relationship between you and your son...if you had to single out one thing—right now. What would that be?

GRANDMA: (She responds quickly and sadly) Nothing! There's nothing! We've come so far apart that there is nothing, nothing! I've traveled all over. I've traveled a lot lately. I've seen the change in people. But I can't change. I'm still Louise Caputo, mother of Pat Cooper—and if he doesn't like it...I'm sorry for him.

ME: What would you say is your fondest memory of your son as Pasquale Caputo, while he was growing up or anything over the years that makes you laugh?

GRANDMA: (She is looking down and seems a bit choked up) Well…oh…I have a lot. He was very lovable. When he was seven or eight years old…every time it was his birthday…he would bring forty to fifty kids over the house whether he had money or not. He had to have a party. He loved parties. But in those days I was always pregnant. He didn't like the idea because I couldn't cook for everyone. (She laughs) It was an issue he couldn't understand. He couldn't understand it. That's the way Italians are. They're family people. I came from a big family, sisters and brothers, we were ten all together. We were brought up from a wonderful mother and father. We were very close. I can't understand this business that just because a person has got money—you have to change. You can't! His wife changed, not me.

ME: Did you feel he was different from your other children while he was growing up?

GRANDMA: Well, first when I gave birth to him he cried so much that I was ready to put something in his bottle. I was ready to kill him. He never wanted to sleep…never wanted to sleep. Then when he became fourteen and fifteen, he slept so much that I couldn't even get him out of bed to go to work. He was so weak and run down because he was growing into a man. One day he fell asleep under the bed for two days. (She laughs) His uncle found him under the bed and asked what happened to him. (She continues laughing) I said that I didn't know…he can't get up…he can't get up lately. That's growing up…a beautiful thing…growing up. He was always jolly, always affectionate. And he gave me beautiful grandchildren. Beautiful grandchildren! I got nine all together and I'm so happy…that they're all intelligent and they're all sensible kids. That's all that matters to me.

ME: Do you ever think that the situation might change someday in the future?

GRANDMA: No, it's too late for me. I'm too tired and families always bring quarrelling. Everybody thinks they're better than everybody else. I couldn't take that anymore. Because I'm still Louise Caputo...my habits can't change. I still like to cook and clean and do things like that. And I like to please my grandchildren. If they need me, they're all welcome to me. I've been lucky enough that I got grandchildren that take me all over. I got one grandson that took me to the Palladium, and I'm an old lady. I felt so good. I felt like a young girl. I say, isn't that wonderful? That's all good memories, very good memories. I got another grandson that takes me to all the best theatre. I say, who could ask for more? Who can ask for any more?

ME: When you hear Pat Cooper on the radio he always sounds angry and bitter toward other entertainers. Was he always this bitter?

GRANDMA: No, no he never was bitter. I guess life in that business makes you bitter. You know its doggie-dog. I say you can't blame him either; they always want to cut his salary and that gives him a lot of aggravation. I know show business is not easy and he's really got a problem, because he's fighting a world of his own. They all do, I say. They can't help it. They can't help it. They become different people. They really do. That's all I could say.

ME: If someone was to come to you tomorrow, ring your bell, come in and say, "Louise, I would like to write a book about your son, about your family, about you growing up...and tell the whole story." Would you want to do that now?

GRANDMA: No, (with sadness in her voice) I don't think I'd like to go through that again. I says, it wasn't interesting...I didn't have a youth...I had three children in five years and another two after that. My youth was gone. I was already miserable because we had no money, my husband made nothing, and to grow up in an environment like that...I don't think I could take it anymore. No, I've had it. I've had it with everybody.

ME: And about this interview that we're doing now. What or how come you agreed to do an interview like this?

GRANDMA: Well, I figured it's helping my grandson. That's all I'm interested in. If he's happy...I'm happy. I says, I can help any of my grandchildren. I helped Patty, I helped my daughters, and I helped everybody. So, if they need me, I'm there. That's all I live for.

ME: Getting back to that book idea. If there was a book written and it was just about to be completed...in the last chapter or even the last page...something you want to say to maybe your son, to the people. What would that be? The last paragraph, the last thought, anything on your mind.

GRANDMA: Well...I'll always say that, 'I love you, Patty,' whether you're Pat Cooper or not, you're still my son. And I hold no grudge against you or nothing. I just hope you're happy. That's all that matters.

ME: It's been really wonderful. Thank you very much for being here. We thank you Louise. We thank you. I'm Michael Caputo. Goodbye. (I waited a few seconds, then stood up and kissed her)

My project was a big hit at school and with the family. Not everybody in the class knew who Pat Cooper was, but after that day they all knew who my grandmother was. And they fell in love with her. I cherished that interview! At that time I really thought it might go somewhere, maybe not prime time, but perhaps something in the media. I wanted to let the world know the truth about the situation with my father, straight from his mother's mouth. I ended up just copyrighting it and had high hopes that it would come in handy someday.

After the interview, I made a concerted effort to get a job. I was enthusiastic at first and used the school's placement service for some leads. I tried for months with them, but was left frustrated. Nobody ever told me when I registered that I would have to start in a smaller market first. I knew if I left the city I'd be miserable and with a heavy accent like mine, I'd never be put on the air. Besides, I didn't want to leave my friends and family. If I was going to leave New York it would be for an acting career and nothing else.

That year I felt more confused than ever. I felt like I was reliving my teenage years all over again, except now I was almost thirty. The majority of my twenties were spent taking classes and attending different schools. I had a lot of training and really thought by this time I'd be working in some aspect of the business. The whole purpose of going to the Center for Media Arts was to have something else to fall back on. One of my biggest fears was becoming a reality; that I'd be stuck working in a flower shop for the rest of my life.

Everything was coming to a head that year, even the situation with my father. One night I got into a tiff with his wife Patti at Dangerfield's comedy club. As soon as I walked into the place I ran into her. She was sitting at a table by the entrance to the club with her baby daughter Patti Jo and some well-dressed middle aged man. He could have been related to her or just a business associate of my father's. I wasn't sure because she never introduced him to me. I immediately walked over and attempted to kiss her hello. For no apparent reason she turned her face away from me. "Why are you such a troublemaker? You're just like Alexis is…on Dynasty!" I said with disgust. She didn't say a word, but responded with a look like she was highly offended. Then she grabbed Patti Jo, and this time she turned her back on me. I quickly gave her my back, too, and then went to go look for my father.

When I walked into the main room, he was about to go on stage. I don't know if he saw me, but I stood in the back for half the show. I was too upset to stay any longer. All I kept thinking about was how she snubbed me. She was blatantly rude to me, for no reason, in front of that strange man and her daughter. She really pissed me off and treated me like I was garbage. It was so humiliating. All I wanted to do was surprise my father and she had to start something. It never failed. Every time I dropped by—without calling him first; something would go wrong. I didn't think his wife would be there and if I knew that I wouldn't have gone. She always made me feel uncomfortable and never looked happy to see me. Her behavior that night was uncalled for and proved, once again, how she really felt about me. I should have seen it coming. I found out a couple of years later that she told my father I called her a whore. I don't know where she got that from and why she twisted the story, but she successfully managed to put a bigger wedge between him and me. Of course he believed her, and years later threw it in my face. I never heard the end of it. He didn't even call and ask me what happened that night. Instead, he just believed her and held a grudge. I was fed up and after that night I promised myself that I was done with them, once and for all.

Shortly after the incident at Dangerfield's I ran into my grandfather—of all people, on the "F" train. I was on the way to my grandmother's house when all of a sudden he walked in and sat down directly across the way from me. What were the chances of that happening? I had only seen my grandfather four times in my life and that was probably the fourth time. He had aged so much and looked very frail. My immediate reaction was to say, "Grandpa is that you." But something kept me in my seat. I wanted to see if he knew who I was. I wanted to see if he recognized me first. And if he did, would he say hello. We played the staring game for about three or four stops. By the expression on his face, I knew that I looked familiar to him. But he said nothing and continued to stare at me. I was pretty sure it was him, and if he got off at the Carroll Street stop, then I'd know for sure. I sat there thinking how pathetic it was that my own grandfather didn't recognize me. But that was his choice, just like my father's. He decided early on not to be a part of our lives. And my father ended up doing the same exact thing. I was disgusted with the both of them. I could only imagine how my grandmother felt.

As we pulled into the Carroll Street station I realized my suspicion was right; it was grandpa. He slowly lifted himself up and held on until the train completely stopped. As he exited the car he glanced back at me one last time. I watched him as we pulled away, wondering why he didn't bother to say hello. But, who knows? He was probably thinking the same thing about me.

I couldn't wait to get to my grandmother's house and tell her that I ran into him. She was surprised that I didn't say hello, but understood why. That was the first time we really discussed my grandfather. It was also the last time I would see him alive. He died later that year on the same day as my grandmother's birthday. I was dead set against going to his wake or the funeral, and nobody forced me to go. I changed my mind at the last minute only out of respect for my grandmother.

My father never came to the wake or the funeral. He didn't send flowers or a mass card, and never called the family to acknowledge his fathers passing. I wasn't surprised and couldn't help but wonder; if I died tomorrow would he come to mine?

Chapter Eight

- Family Affair -

I was sick and tired of trying to figure everything out. It was one thing after another: my job, my father and my non-existing career. It wasn't my nature to just pick up and go, but with the circumstances the way they were I felt I needed to get away from it all. I decided to move to the west coast, literally overnight. I had just celebrated my thirtieth birthday and figured it was now or never if I really wanted to have an acting career. If Broadway couldn't use me then maybe Hollywood could.

The hardest part of it all was leaving my family and friends behind. My mother was worried and at first tried to talk me out of it. My grandmother said I would hate California. The only person that understood was my friend Bill. He helped me pack up everything and even found a couple to take over my apartment. It was funny because he got me into the building and now he was the person that would get me out. He knew a couple that wanted my apartment and said they might be interested in buying everything in it, too. By the end of the week they wrote me out a check for one lump sum and the deal was done. Within a month I was living in Manhattan with my favorite cousin Judy. I stayed with her up until the holidays and it turned out to be the most exciting three months I had that year. I felt like I was on a long vacation and it was during that time I quit my job. That was the best part! Then for the last week in December I went back to Brooklyn one last time to stay with my friends. They gave me a wonderful farewell party and promised to come visit me. I spent a quiet New Year's Eve on Long Island with my mother and my sister. And then the next morning they drove me to the airport.

After saying goodbye at the terminal, my teary-eyed mother and sister watched me as I slowly walked down the long corridor.

The next time I would see them would be in July for my sister's wedding. It was a long flight and I spent most of my time reading a book called, "The Road Less Traveled." The perfect book to read in route to my new life.

When I arrived in Los Angeles I was very fortunate to find everything that I needed within the first month: a job, a place to live, a car and even a gym. I learned the street names and the neighborhoods by taking little drives everyday. Except for a cousin who lived in the valley, I was on my own. He showed me around a couple of times and helped familiarize me with some of the good restaurants.

I rented a small studio in Hollywood that had a swimming pool and a parking garage. I didn't have to think twice about taking that place. The job was another story. I was hired as a parking attendant for one of the popular hotels. The tips were great, the cars were incredible and the hours were perfect. But there was one problem: I didn't know how to drive a stick shift. I faked it for as long as I could and then I just gave up. I even took a couple of classes at some local driving school, but I still couldn't get used to that clutch. Finally I quit after three weeks because I was afraid of ruining somebody's car.

The next job I found was out of a local West Hollywood newspaper. I came across a company that was looking for a phone operator and customer service representative. I knew I had this job before I even got there, especially with all my experience from the flower shop. Besides, I was a New Yorker and they usually liked that. The office was very informal and I was the only one sitting there wearing a jacket and tie. When the guy finished interviewing me and I found out the full description of the job, I almost burst out laughing in his face. They were looking for a phone sex operator to work the evening shift. Phone sex was very popular back then and I didn't realize how popular it was until I started working there. I began at six o'clock in the evening and manned the telephones until one o'clock in the morning. They'd be ringing off the hook with horny people from all over the country who were looking to fulfill their fantasies. My job was to take down their credit card information and pre-interview them to find out exactly what they wanted. The whole process took less than five minutes. Once the credit card was approved then I would call up one of our actors and give him the specifics. He would then call the client back and act out the fantasy. The more talented the actors the more repeat clients they had. And that meant more money and hefty tips. We usually had five or six actors on a night and some of them were really good.

Now that I had landed a full time job everything else fell into place. I began taking a monologue class at the Actors Center. The teacher was very knowledgeable and suggested some good material for me. At the end of the course she videotaped my work and critiqued it. I wasn't happy about being in school again, but I knew it was the only way to make some connections. Furthermore, I needed to get some new material together before I started auditioning.

My friends Bill and Bob came to visit me in the middle of April. They kept me company for a week and we went all over the place. It was good to see them and they came at the perfect time. California was more spread out than New York and I found it difficult to make friends. I only had a few acquaintances from the school but no one that I really felt close to. I found that most people in L.A. were into their own thing and spent more time in the car than anywhere else. Nobody hung out on the streets like they did in Brooklyn. There was a weird vibe in the air that I just couldn't get used to. I was feeling lonely and having second thoughts.

My friends enjoyed themselves, especially the day we went sightseeing to the stars homes. Bob had to see Engelbert Humperdinck's house. Bill had to see Sonny and Cher's. Then after all the excitement, I showed them where Barbra Streisand lived. It was hysterical and we were lucky that we didn't get arrested. We were peeking over the wall by Engelbert's house and his daughter caught us. She was very sweet and started talking to my friends. I thought Bob was going to have heart failure; he was so infatuated with her. I couldn't blame him. We were all star struck and I would have been the same way if that was Barbra Streisand's son. She made his day and that was the highlight of their vacation.

When my friends left I was homesick. I didn't know what to do with myself. For a week it was just like old times again. I missed Brooklyn, my friends and my family. This was the longest amount of time I had ever been away from home. But now this was home and I had a hard time adjusting to it. At that moment if I could have reversed everything I would have. Everyone told me to check it out first to see if I would like it. But I had my mind made up, I acted impulsively, and nobody could have talked me out of it, anyway. I had to stay focused on the reason why I went out there in the first place. And that was to become an actor. Suddenly that didn't seem that important to me anymore and I didn't know why.

I finally made up my mind to go back to New York, after seeing the movie, "Moonstruck." That flick brought back so many memories that I left the theatre crying. When I got back to my apartment I called my mother and told her that I was coming home. She didn't sound surprised at all. It was almost as if she knew. The following week I bought a one-way ticket to New York and made arrangements to ship my car back. I would arrive home a month later and just in time for my sister's wedding.

It was the greatest feeling in the world being home, and after a few weeks it felt like I never left. I didn't want to go back to the Garden Path, but that's where I ended up. It was the only job that would pay me a decent salary and they wanted me back. I felt like such a failure when I returned and got the impression that they were laughing at me behind my back. It might have been my imagination, but that's the way some of them were in that store. After all, they thought when I went to California I'd become a star. And when I left, so did I.

My sister's wedding was an awesome celebration and the church ceremony was extra special because I had the honor of giving her away. The thing I remember most about her wedding day—besides the fact that she made such a beautiful bride, was what she did for me at the reception hall. She had the band play my favorite song. We slow danced and embraced to, "The Way We Were," while everyone took pictures and videotaped us. For me that was the highlight of the evening and I felt so good. I was home!

At this point I was living with my mother in Long Island and trying to recoup the money I had spent from my move to Los Angeles. One morning in late summer after my mother had left for work I was laying down in bed debating whether I wanted to get up or not. I felt myself drifting in and out of consciousness when the telephone rang. I jumped out of bed on the third ring. It was my friend Bill and his tone was urgent. "Hurry, Mike...turn on the radio! Your father's bad mouthing your whole family: your grandmother, your sister, your aunts, everyone. He's a guest on the Howard Stern show."

I never listened to talk radio and had no idea who Howard Stern was. Bill was a big fan and listened to his show every morning on his way into work. He even had a radio on his desk so he wouldn't miss a word. My hands began to shake as I fiddled with the dial searching for my father's voice. I was so nervous; I couldn't even find the damn station. At the same time Bill was screaming in my ear, "92K Rock...92.3K Rock, Mike...hurry! Oh shit, they just went to a commercial. What are you doing? Why don't you call the show and tell them that you're Pat's son...and Howard will put you on the air."

"Are you serious? They won't put me on...I'm nobody...they're not just going to let me on the radio for nothing. What am I going to say to them anyway?" I said.

"Just tell them you're Pat Cooper's son and that you want to tell your side of the story. They'll put you on, Mike...I'm telling you," he said.

That's all I had to hear. My friend said the magic words and told me to call information right away. While I was on the phone with the operator, I popped a blank cassette into my stereo just in case Bill was right. I found the station and heard my father gloating about something. I didn't hear him say anything about anyone in particular, but I believed my friend and proceeded to call the station anyway. My father was always saying something derogatory about the family and Bill wasn't the first person who told me that.

I could hear them transferring me from line to line and then placing me on hold. My heart was still pounding. I spoke with a few different people on the phone and told them all the same thing: That I was Pat Cooper's son and that I had something to say. At first they were leery with the phone call; they didn't believe that I was his son.

Once Howard got on the phone and introduced himself, I pressed in the record button on the stereo and knew in a couple of seconds I would be on the air. In the background I could hear a few other voices, one was my father's and the other one was Robin's, Howard's sidekick on the show. For the first couple of minutes I was nervous and you could hear it in my voice. There was a little confusion at first and then once my father confirmed that it was me, he said hello. The first words I said to him were: How are you? That was the way I began all our phone conversations ever since he made a big fuss with me about phone etiquette years ago.

Howard began the interview with a general comment. My father told him that the last time we saw each other was five years ago when I asked him for some money. That was way off base and immediately put me on the defensive. The last time I asked my father for anything was around my eighteenth birthday, which was fourteen years ago. And that wasn't the last time I'd seen him, either. I remember feeling hurt that I had to ask for a gift in the first place and I pledged from that day on never to bother asking him anymore. Only a minute on the radio and already the shit was flying.

The next question from Stern was a loaded one and it carried through the rest of the show. They wanted me to explain what happened between my father and I. I felt like saying: Why don't you ask my father that question? All my life I tried to figure out why other kids, who were in the same situation as my sister and I, managed to sustain a relationship with their fathers.

"Just because you're divorcing your wife doesn't mean you're divorcing your children, too. What ever happened between me and my father seemed to have happened with my father and the rest of the family also," I said.

[I tried to explain further, but my father interrupted.]

"Didn't you ask your mother...'why is my father so bad?' Don't you ask questions? 'Why are you putting my father in the toilet, ma?'" he said.

[For the next few minutes I had to listen to my father rationalize his behavior and blame my mother. It was the same excuse that he had alluded to before. He was trying to convince the audience and himself that if my mother didn't pollute our minds he would have had a better relationship with us. The only person my father had to blame for the bad relationship or the non-existing one was himself.]

He carried on, raising his voice, that I should have challenged my mother regardless of my age. He went off on a million tangents and brought up the alimony checks again. It still bothered him that he had to always mail the checks through the court system for twenty-one years. I challenged him and told him that had nothing to do with my sister and I.

The conversation was getting a little hot. My father was crazed and everyone was talking at the same time. It was then that I realized there were more than three people in the studio. Howard tried to make light of the situation and suggested that my father and I get together. He also cracked a few jokes and used them to try and calm my father down a bit. Nothing worked. Everybody had different opinions, but they all agreed with me when I said that I was a "victim of circumstance."

[There were about thirty seconds of normality in the room and then my father got all worked up again.]

"I'm hurt because people come to me that know them and say, 'How can you be so bad to these kids? They're so good,'" he said.

"You see…you see that? What does that have to do with me?" I said defensively.

"It has a lot to do with you, Mike because you stand there and let them say that. Whether you hang out with them or not, they're still your family and you should tell them to back off. 'Don't embarrass my father. And if you don't like it…he's still my father and you can kiss my butt!'"

[After that presumptuous remark we really got into it. I was pissed off and finally got the courage to say to him what I had wanted to say to him for years. I felt safe in that arena knowing that the deejays and the audience would be like the judge and the jury. There would be no slamming the phone down this time.]

"How do you know whether I said that or not…how do you know I don't say that?" I questioned him.
"Because I know you're not the kind of guy to do that."
"How do you know? How do you know?" I shouted at him repeatedly.
"Because you go which way the wind shifts," he said sarcastically.
"How do you know what kind of guy I am because you haven't been around for the last thirty-two years?" I said furiously.
"I haven't been around for thirty two years?" He said, as if I was lying.

"You don't know who I am!" I shouted.

"Mike, I've been in your company many times."

"You don't know who I am!"

"Yes I do. I absolutely do."

"That's the problem...he doesn't know who I am...he thinks he knows who I am!" I shouted repeatedly.

[It felt good to finally get that off my chest. For the next few minutes my father continued to defend his absence. It sounded like he was reading from a script. Who was this stranger? Was this man my father or was he just being Pat Cooper again? He brought up the money issue again and again, and said that's all I ever wanted from him. When I heard that I lost it. I screamed into the telephone at the top of my lungs hoping he would get it this time.]

"I don't want you for your money...get that into your head! I don't need you for your money!"

[After that outburst he changed the subject back to the family stuff. He wanted me to ask my grandmother why she treated him, an only son, like a second class citizen. He demanded that I be the mediator, not only with her, but with the rest of the family, too. I downright refused and told him that he needed to take care of those issues himself. He didn't like that answer and said I was "copping out." My father expected me to do his dirty work and I made him understand that I didn't want any part of it.]

In the midst of all the confusion I heard somebody in the background ask my father if he loved me. Stuttering and a bit shaken he replied that he did. Another guest on the show dared him to tell me. The whole room got quiet. After he told me everyone started clapping and cheering. That was the first time I had ever heard him say those words to me. I didn't know what to think and felt uncomfortable with it, strangely enough. Then it was my turn. Once I proclaimed my love everyone began clapping and cheering again. We made some progress and before I got off the phone my father agreed to call me and make plans to go to dinner. I even mentioned that I wanted to pay for it to show everyone that my intentions were sincere. I thought that was the end of the conversation until somebody made another comment that triggered my father off again.

For another ten minutes he continued to knock the family. This time he was more belligerent and said that I took their side. He said they were jealous of his success and that we were all looking for a piece of the pie. He reiterated everything that he said earlier and then some. I felt like throwing up. He sounded like a broken record. This was his reality and I was tired of being put in the middle of it. It was the same crap I used to hear when we went to dinner and one of the main reasons why I stopped going. I was sick of hearing it, and realized that this was the stuff he held against me. He wasn't even ashamed to say it on the radio. Despite all that rigmarole, we concluded our debate on a peaceful note and he promised to call me.

When I hung up the phone my head was spinning. I had lost all sense of time. I felt exhilarated and empowered because I had finally said some of the things I've wanted to say to him for years. Also, it was the longest conversation we ever had. The Howard Stern Show had given me the forum to speak my mind and for that I am forever grateful. With the help of the show I had made it to first base; a home run would be another story. Could we really have a relationship after so many years? Would the upcoming dinner date be another waste of time? I sat there daydreaming about all the possibilities, good and bad. How wonderful it would be if this radio show could really turn this thing around.

Impulsively, I decided to call my sister. I was curious to hear what she had to say about everything. She had no relationship with him whatsoever and her situation was worse than mine. I gave her a brief synopsis of what happened and before I could finish she said she wanted to call. I told her how ruthless he had been with me and tried to warn her. But she still insisted. After all, she was his daughter and had every right to get things off her chest, too. After being introduced to the airwaves she immediately confronted her father.

"Yes…hello. Is my father there? I'd like to know what he has to say to me after twelve years," she said.

"I don't have nothing to say to you after twelve years," he said.
"Well, I have a lot to say after twelve years," she said.
"You can say anything you want and I respect your right to say it," he said.

[My sister's opening statement had to do with his routine and her career. She told him she didn't want him to joke or make demeaning statements about her teaching profession anymore. He tried convincing her that when he joked about teachers it was a generality that had nothing to do with her at all; it was the creative process of comedy that she just didn't understand. She made it clear that she didn't like it and wanted him to stop. Things were calm up until that point. But when she brought up that he was never there for her and that she had to pay her way through college, he went nuts.]

"That's what you're supposed to do…that's what you're supposed to do. You're a lady…that's right…that's right," he yelled at her.

"I paid for everything on my own!" She yelled back at him.
"That's what you're supposed to do," he persisted.
"That's what I'm supposed to do…that's what I'm supposed to do. Did your step-daughter pay for her college education? I doubt it very much," she yelled.
"I don't have a step-daughter. I don't have a step-daughter…back off…back off!" He screamed.
"You didn't adopt a daughter," she asked.
"Back off", he screamed, avoiding her question.

[They went back and forth with this a few times and he refused to talk about his adopted daughter. But my sister pressed him.]

"You didn't adopt a daughter with your other wife," she asked.

"Back off! Don't call my daughter a step-daughter cause you're a fool. You're showing your evil side."

[The conversation got uglier and once she made her point she moved on. She asked him why he didn't go to his father's funeral. That pissed him off some more and he started yelling about that.]

"I didn't see my father for twelve years and I wasn't gonna see him in the funeral parlor," he said.

"Don't you think it's a little strange?"

"No, you're strange…you're strange!"

[Then she brought up grandma.]

"When was the last time you seen your mother?" She asked.

"When she asked me to pay the back rent that I didn't owe."

"Isn't that a disgrace to do to your mother after how many years?"

"I'm a disgrace? You know something…for a school teacher you have no common sense" he said.

"For a grown man you have no common sense."

[Twenty years after the fact my father sent his mother a five-thousand dollar check to cover the six years that we lived in her house rent free. He said that she asked him for it, which I knew was a lie. In a lowdown tactic he was trying to pay her off for taking care of his kids. My grandmother was devastated; it was a smack in the face. After that comment he went back to defending himself saying that he was a righteous man and a gentleman, and that everybody knew that about him—except the family.]

"We're fed up with his nonsense." He comes out smelling like a rose every time. I just want the whole world to know that this man is really a phony...and everything he says...every joke...is a disgrace to his family," she said.

[In less than five minutes they were out of control. Everyone knew that a father and daughter relationship was not happening. It was hopeless and the opinion in the room was that they were hurt. My sister was sickened by his lies and hypocrisy, and she made sure that everyone understood why. My father denied being hurt and said my sister was angry because she had to pay her way through college. She quickly corrected him and said she was angry because he never accepted his responsibility as a father. They were back to square one again and he gave her the same answer he gave me: that he paid his responsibilities and owed us nothing. She proudly reminded him and made sure the audience knew that anything she got in her life was no thanks to him. Then out of nowhere he switched gears and reprimanded her.]

"And don't leave no pineapples at my door!" He warned.
"I can do whatever I want," she said.
"Don't leave no pineapples by my door!" He shouted.

[When my sister went on her honeymoon she left a pineapple at his house to let him know that she just got married. She did that as a kind gesture and he took it as a threat. In her own special way she was telling him that she was happy and that he had missed out on another important day in her life. She was expressing her gratitude to everyone in the family and when she mentioned his mother that set him off again.]

"You know, I'm surprised that my grandmother hasn't called up. My grandmother is very hurt over this situation," she said.
"Your grandmother is not hurt over any situation, cause your grandmother is for your grandmother. And your grandmother never gave her son anything to talk about that's nice," he screamed.

[She interrupted him]

"That's what you say about your mother."

[He continued to yell and upstage her.]

"Your father mailed her a check for five thousand dol-lars…nice man, I am! Huh! Where's the money…that's all yous people know…where's the money!" He said.

"Can I tell you something? You don't know your mother. Your mother is the most wonderful person in the world and you have nothing good to say about her," she said.

[Everybody is talking at the same time and there is total chaos in the room. My father is heard in the background screaming "good-bye" over and over again to try and in-timidate her so she would hang up the phone. That might have happened, but when he brought up money again, she let him have it.]

"I don't need money. Look, money to me…money doesn't buy you love, remember that. Money will not be your comfort. Your family is your comfort. Remember that! Money does not buy hap-piness or health," she stated.

"All right, so…you know what we do. You stay your way and I'll stay my way. That's the way it's gonna be," he said.

"Let me tell you something! I stayed my way seventeen years. You never gave me a damn thing! I never got anything! I never asked you for anything! I don't want your money and I don't want anything from you!" She yelled.

[After that outburst, my sister made him promise never to use her name or even associate any of his jokes with her or her profession. The deejays felt bad that they couldn't work things out. My sister thanked them and said she was grate-ful that she was able to tell the true story. It sounded like she was about to hang up the phone when my father pulled her back into the conversation. He started arguing and

*screamed at her to tell the truth. Challenging him again, she
stated that he left her in a hospital when she was two weeks
old. He went berserk after that.]*

"Who told you that? Who told you that? Answer my question...who told you that?" He screamed and demanded.

*[Giving him a taste of his own medicine, she ignored him
and never answered the question. Instead, she got him to
admit that he was never there for her.]*

"Were you there when I was growing up? Were you there
for any one of my birthdays?" She crisply asked.

"No!" He said.

"Did you ever give me a birthday gift?" She asked.

"No!" He said firmly.

"Were you there for my confirmation, communion, and graduations?" she screamed.

"No...No, I was never there!" He said firmly and proudly.

"Okay! Thank you! You just said you were never there," she
clarified.

"Because you see the way your mouth is...that's why I was
never there," he said.

"You were never there!" She firmly stated.

"That's why I was never there...because you just showed
your character," he lashed back.

"You were never there!" She said repeatedly.

"Because you have no character!" He said.

"But I was a child...I was a child...you were never there!
Now everybody knows the true story!" She proudly stated.

*[That morning my sister became my hero. She finally got him
to admit, in less than fifteen minutes, that he was never there for
us. Even I wasn't able to do that and I was on the radio longer than
she was. I was proud of her and started clapping. He was held
accountable and left with mud on his face. He tried to make excuses like it was a flaw in her personality that kept him away. But
she was a child, we were both children and there was no excuse.]*

Even when she hung up the phone my father continued. He was so flustered; you could hear it clearly coming over the radio. Then all of a sudden he began criticizing my grandmother and making assertions that I knew weren't true. That's when I decided to call her so she could set the record straight herself. It took me a few minutes to explain everything to her, and of course, she was reluctant to call. My grandmother felt the situation was hopeless and said if she called it would only "fan the flames" and make matters worse. Despite that, I gave her the number and the next thing I knew they were announcing her name over the radio.

They checked with my father first before putting her on the air. Before they could even welcome her she blurted out, "He's a wreck!" Everybody in the studio laughed. She agreed that things were a mess and said that her son was very stubborn.

"Can you believe a man who talks about his mother and his family so much…and made millions of dollars on them, suddenly quits. He doesn't want to bother with them, he hates them. They're all after his money. Who cares? Who cares? Money doesn't mean much to me. There's nothing in the world but your health. He thinks money is important. It's not!" She said.

[My father calmly denies her accusations and they begin on a sour note.]

"I never said money was important, number one. Number two, what my mother doesn't seem to realize is that I brought this up. If I wasn't concerned I wouldn't have brought this up today…"

[My grandmother is heard calling him a liar in the background. My father is ignoring her and trying to remain cool while explaining himself to the audience. He is referring to something he said earlier and off on some other tangent. They are talking at the same time and it's difficult to understand what they're both saying. Then my grandmother raised her voice.]

160

"You were never concerned! Tell the truth!" She demanded.

"I did tell the truth," he answered.

"You never told the truth, in your whole life!" She yelled.

"I got nothing to hide. I'm not ashamed. Cause you know why? I know what I've done and what I said was the right thing for me. And I didn't intentionally go to hurt them, or to kill them, or to stab them," he said.

[Cutting him off, she yelled]

"It would have been better. It would have been better if you stabbed me!"

[After that comment my father snapped, and then it was World War III.]

"See, now she wants you to stab her. Now she wants to be the mother. Now today she's gonna be my mother. Yesterday she's not my mother. When I was three years in the street...where was my mother? Ask her where my mother was? But I didn't say nothing. I didn't give her my problems. I didn't ask them to give me a loan," he said.

"God have mercy on him...God have mercy on him," she pleaded.

"Look at this, 'God have mercy on him.' I don't want nothing from her!" He screamed.

[He rambled on for the next couple of minutes about the past and what she did and didn't do in his life. Most of the things that followed were shameful and sad.]

"See they feel they gotta get paid cause you mention the word mother or father or sister or daughter. You have to pay them. Look what...we made you successful they're telling you...I speak well about my mother and father on that stage!" He shouted.

"Because you made money on them," she answered.

"Did you hear what she just said?"

"On my life you made money," she shouted.

161

"On her life I made money. You never turned a saint upside down in your life, mother. So don't con me. You ought to be ashamed of yourself," he snapped.

[Things were out of control. Even Howard wasn't able to placate my father, but he managed to quiet things down for a few seconds. He used that time to apologize to my grandmother for not being able to resolve any of the issues. My grandmother told him that her son was a liar and that his attitude was an ongoing problem. That's when my father blew up again and viciously attacked her. He brought up grandpa and the reason why he didn't go to the funeral. She told him to forgive and forget. He whined that his father was never there for him and that she never did anything for him either. Grandma reminded him that she took care of his kids for ten years. He threw the back-rent check in her face again and twisted the story. It was one low-blow after another. He asked her if she wanted to be paid for the food and clothes she gave us, too. She blasted him for even thinking that. He was relentless and cruel, and it got worse.]

"I earned my money…dear mother! I earned it and not by you," he said.

"So did I, so did I!" She shouted back.

"Then keep it! I don't want yours. Keep it! Give it to your grandkids. They deserve it," he shouted.

"Ten years…I took care of your children." she said.

"You're supposed to. You're a grandmother. You're supposed to. That's your chore in life!" He shouted.

"Everybody's supposed to. What about you?" She asked.

"I've done my thing. I've done my duty," he proclaimed.

"Where's your duty as a father?" She asked.

"My duty as a father is not being bulldozed by my kids. And not being conned by my kids.

"Oh cut it out! You're the only one that bulldozes everybody," she said.

[He continued bullying her with his provocative remarks until she got disgusted and finally hung up.]

"Take your daughter-in-laws side. Take your daughter-in-laws side. You don't like men. You never liked men. Anything with pants you can't handle. Remember that! Anything with pants...you're the man and the woman in the family. Go to your daughters...kiss your daughters!"

"See the type he is. You can't control him. He loves trouble," she said.

"Goodbye...goodbye...wish you luck!" He shouted.

"He loves trouble, he loves trouble," she repeated.

"Yeah...you're the troublemaker, miss!" He said.

"You're the troublemaker!" She shouted.

[That was the end of their radio conversation and the last time they ever spoke.]

Once I heard those clicks it was over. I didn't know whether to cry or to jump for joy. My grandmother had held her own and I was proud of her, but I still felt guilty that I made her call. She said it was going to end that way, and it did.

After that they went to a commercial break and I just sat there in my room totally consumed. What would come of this and what the hell just happened? When they returned my father kept apologizing to the radio station for taking up so much air time. He left the show that morning knocking his sisters and saying that it was impossible to love them or any of us because we were all money hungry.

As soon as the show went off the air the phone rang. I thought it was my grandmother or my sister, but it was Bill. I thanked him a hundred times for persuading me to call in, and we both agreed that fate had a funny way of making things happen. I told him it was the closest thing to group therapy except that millions of people were listening. I rushed him off the phone when he mentioned my grandmother. I was worried about her and meant to call her before the phone rang. She was eighty-two at the time and all I needed was for her to have a heart attack on me. When I called there was no answer. At first I panicked, but then I remembered what she used to say: "When you're nervous or got things on your mind, stop in church and talk to God. It'll do you a world of good." So I assumed she was safe in church. I took a couple of deep breaths with that thought in mind and then called my mother. When I gave her the rundown she was shocked. She made me leave the cassette in the stereo so that she could listen to it as soon as she got home.

When I got to work I was surprised that everyone knew already. My bosses told me that people were calling the store all day to try and reach me. That's when I realized I mentioned the name of the florist over the air. What a mistake that was. Some even left their phone numbers expecting me to call them back. It was like a zoo in there and I felt like running home. I ended up on the phone all night discussing everything. First I called a few of the people back because I was curious to see what they wanted. Some were praising me for having courage while others were sympathetic and gave their advice. All in all they were supportive and wished me luck. When I called my mother she sounded overly concerned. She was doubtful and questioned whether this would do me any good. It was unsettling for her and she felt rehashing it would only have further emotional repercussions for everyone.

When I got home we continued our discussion and I had to reassure her that everything was going to be okay. We listened to parts of the tape and then I went to bed. All night I tossed and turned and dwelled on everything again. I remember talking to God and thanking him for making this happen. Finally, I had a voice. Then I rolled over and fell asleep.

Early the next morning I turned on the radio to see if my father was on again. I could hear Howard taking calls and he seemed overwhelmed. Everyone had something to say about my family and the outcome of the show. Some of the comments were negative and some were positive. One guy even thought the whole thing was staged. That was totally ridiculous and I was glad that Stern hung up on him. Anyone could tell that was reality radio and the best part was it happened all by accident. It was fascinating to hear so many different points of view.

When I realized my father wasn't there and wasn't calling in, I started to get a little edgy. How did he expect us to get together? He didn't have my phone number and I didn't have his. He never would have remembered the name of the place where I worked, even though I mentioned it on the air just a day before. That's when I decided to call the radio station and get his number. While I was on the phone with them, my father called in, and by seven-thirty we were both on the air again. His monotonous speech went on for almost ten minutes straight and I couldn't get a word in edgewise until he finished with his repugnant conclusions. Yesterday was judgment day for him. Today it sounded like he was giving a review and on the verge of a nervous breakdown.

[He opened his monologue speaking calmly, but warning me.]

"Hey Mike, don't ever say to people that for two years you never found me. That's the lowest lie. I never hid out. I got records and dates to prove I was there. I paid your mother forty dollars a week...I was making sixty. Then it went to sixty-five dollars...then it went to a hundred and thirty dollars. And I'm telling you like a friend not like a father, your mother's lying to you...and what hurts me is that I tried yesterday to open dialogue, but not one person on that side realized that...I used the Howard Stern Show unintentionally and all I heard from all of you was garbage!"

[The more he talked about it, the more worked up he got. Then he started with his mother.]

"You know when I heard from them? The day after I did the Jackie Gleason Show. She said, 'That's my son!' She never said that to me in person...only when I was on Jackie Gleason. She goes to the senior citizen's center and says, 'I'm Mrs. Cooper...' Mr. Mother out there, I'm ashamed of you. I speak for a lot of men and women who want to tell their mother that. I'm ashamed of you and back off!"

[Next it was my sister]

"My daughter came off as a witch, an intelligent witch. She has no street smarts, she's not a nice girl and identical to her mother. I'll step on my daughter for calling my other daughter a step-daughter and my wife a whore. How dare her! That whole family calls my wife a whore. Only the Caputos' are the blessed mothers. How dare them!"

[Then he went nuts because I called up the radio show prematurely and told them that he didn't call me like he promised.]

"What a shower I took yesterday! What a shower! I gave them a chance and they blew it. And my darling son the reason I didn't call you is that I gotta make a living; l.i.v.i.n.g. (he spelled it out) I was gonna call you, but you want it to happen now. I'll call you when I'm ready! I may not be mentally ready to talk to you right away. Gimme a chance to breath! This is an emotional moment for me, son! Son! And I'm a human being, son! And I bleed, son! And I'm telling you right now! Your father has rights, God damn it! And back off! And once in a while say to people in the streets: 'My father is a human being. I don't like him and I don't love him, but he's a human being.' Damn it! I was there. I never ran away. Your mother lied to you. How dare that woman say I hid from her! You can't hide from witches! How dare they insult my intelligence!"

[I interrupted him at that point, but he would only let me get in a few words.]

"I didn't say he wasn't going to call me..." I said. (Barely audible)

"Hey son, I know you better than yourself. You play two ends to the middle. You're a cutie! You're a cutie, but you're not gonna be a cutie with your father...because I got news for you. You better make a stand! I'm either a father on my terms or no father at all...or get yourself somebody else to con because you're not gonna con me. I'm your father. First of all even if I'm not your father, I'm older than you. And you respect my age or I'll sit on your lap!"

[After he was done telling me off he remained hostile and continued to defend himself. My father called us all idiots and then started bragging that he was the ultimate philanthropist. He brought up my grandparents' marriage and said the reason for their divorce was because my grandmother was sneaky with her money. If Howard didn't intervene and remind us about our dinner date he would have screamed his head off for another hour.]

Before getting off the air my father told me to get his phone number from the producer and to call him at the end of the week. Again I had to make the first move. After I hung up I listened to the show for another fifteen minutes. The deejays were busy taking a poll and joking amongst themselves about which one of us would make peace with my father first. Their comments were funny and they went so far as to say they wanted to book us and send us out on tour. I had a good laugh, but knew that would never happen— not in a million years.

The next morning I woke up to a song parody. They used excerpts from our dialogue and joked about it half the morning. I thought it was hysterical. That whole week we were the topic of conversation and I became obsessed with the show. By the time the weekend rolled around I was mentally exhausted.

Friday night I called my father to make plans to meet him on Sunday in front of the World Trade Center. I was looking forward to a peaceful dinner in Little Italy and hoping that we could have a regular normal conversation without bringing the rest of the family into it. Maybe we'll have that heart-to-heart talk that I always wanted. If this turns out to be another bullshit dinner I'll leave him sitting there by himself. I swore to God I would.

Not everyone was thrilled with the outcome of the show. My aunt called me at work and told me to stop calling. She was upset with everything and said my grandmother was too old and couldn't take it. She was worried that something could happen to her as a result of all the sudden media attention combined with the aggravation from my father. I made it clear that my intention was to get my father and her mother talking again; that I had plans to try and get him over grandma's house on Sunday after we had dinner. But she was too upset and didn't want to hear it.

When I arrived home that night my mother wasn't too happy either. She also told me to stop calling the show and to cool it for a while. My mother wanted it to die down because she was embarrassed that everyone knew her business. She also added that my sister was agitated and ashamed to face her students. I snapped back at my mother and reminded her that my sister was the one who insisted on calling. I went to bed annoyed as hell that night because of all the backlash and negative reactions that I never expected.

My father wasn't the only one who took a shower that day. We all did. It took thirty years for this situation to come to a head and it wasn't my fault that the water got too hot for everybody. For me it was therapeutic and a major opportunity. It certainly would have been easier on everybody if it could have been done in a more diplomatic fashion. But that was impossible with the nature of the show and my father's disposition. While everyone was busy coming down on me they had forgotten the real reason why I called the radio in the first place—which was to give "those people" a voice. My father had always referred to everyone in the family, including myself as, "those people." He had been lying to people for years about all of us and it was time the world heard the truth.

For years I had been trying to do that. That was the whole purpose of my school project with my grandmother three years ago and why I persuaded her to call the radio that morning. I wanted to show the world exactly who he really was and that his stage persona was a parody. That day on the radio I got my wish. With one phone call I was able to introduce more than a million listeners to the real Pat Cooper.

Chapter Nine

- Sympathy for the Devil -

I never regretted calling the Howard Stern show nor was I ever sorry with the way things turned out. My sister, on the other hand, wasn't thrilled with the outcome because she didn't realize there would be a painful price for her fifteen minutes of fame. My grandmother never said a word to me about it. I think she looked at the bigger picture; a chance for me to get all this crap off my chest and work though my relationship issues with my father. She wasn't upset with me like everybody else because if she was—believe me, I would have heard about it.

The dinner with my father that Sunday after the show proved to be quite interesting. I had nervously anticipated our get-together wondering if it would be a waste of time. Even though he promised not to bring up the family again, he got on the subject anyway. I thought for sure the revelation he supposedly had that week would have humbled him, but I was wrong. He was arrogant and unashamed of his behavior on the show and made it clear that his perspectives would never change. He was like a stubborn kid in the middle of a never-ending tantrum. My grandmother was right; he had a one track-mind and was impossible. I was so frustrated with his bullshit and I should've left him in the restaurant like I said I was going to. That dinner in Little Italy was our last supper.

Within two weeks everything died down. I eventually stopped listening to the show and lost all desire to call, whether my father was on or not. It was time to get back on with my life and to stop relentlessly pursuing him. My idea of a relationship was more than just having a dinner with him every couple of years. I had done that as far back as I could remember and I was frustrated and angry that he wouldn't give me anything more. I thought my radio debut would've woken him up, but it didn't.

The following week I registered with a few real estate brokers. I found a beautiful apartment in a new rent-stabilized building in Manhattan. I lucked out! I had been living at home with my mother for over a year and it was great, but I needed to get my own place again. She felt bad to see me go and I have to admit it was harder to leave home the second time around, especially now that she was alone.

Once I settled in I concentrated on looking for a different job. This time I was going to make sure that I got out of that florist for good. The Center for Media Arts had a lifetime placement division and I dropped by to see if they could find me something or give me a few leads. Somebody there suggested that I do an internship at one of the local television studios to get my foot in the door. It didn't take me long to find out that most of the talk shows were based in New York and conveniently within walking distance from my new apartment.

I finally got a break and landed a gig as an intern on the Geraldo Rivera show. I worked with the Geraldo team for a few hours a day, then after that I'd hop on the subway and head straight down to my paying job. It was a pretty hectic schedule, but I loved it. It was an education being an intern at that place and I learned more in three months than I did in a year's time at school. The first month I was a gofer doing a little bit of everything for everybody in the office. After seeing how motivated and eager I was they put me to use around the studio more. That's when I really learned the business. I was lucky to be able to observe and work closely with the staff in the control room. The director with his technical commands and wizardry supervised the taping of five to seven shows a week. Everything and everyone depended on him and the final result was flawless. I used to leave there every day fascinated and proud to be part of that team. Now, if only they would hire me.

One day at the office my curiosity led me into the conference room. I knew there was an over-sized calendar hanging on the wall with the names of the upcoming shows for the month. I never really paid much attention to it, but I knew about sweeps week and I wanted to see what the themes were going to be. Everything was all about ratings in that business and New York was a very competitive market. The Geraldo Rivera talk show wasn't the only game in town and for that reason alone things had to be planned ahead of time and orchestrated very carefully. One of the titles that caught my eye that day was: "Can Fatherhood be Forced?" The minute I saw that I stopped breathing. Just when I started to forget about my father and move on with my life, this shit hits me in the face. It got me thinking; this had to be more than just a coincidence. This had to be God or something telling me to give him another chance. Nobody there knew I was Pat Cooper's son or that I had been on the Howard Stern show four months earlier with the same issue. It was time to let them know.

Without even thinking any further, I ran over to the producer and told her who I was. Before saying anything she handed me a piece of paper from her desk to show me that she had the words "Pat Cooper family" scribbled on it. Now, there was no doubt in my mind that this was meant to be. She had relentlessly tried to contact us for weeks, and the whole time I was right under her nose. If that wasn't fate than nothing was! After the initial shock we talked business. I told her right up front that I was interested in doing a segment. But she still wanted me to go home and think about it first. This was a nationwide television show and a whole different ball game than radio. She wanted to make sure that I understood that. I had nothing to think about; my mind was already made up. Little did she know I had wanted to do this for years. It would be the ultimate chance to confront my father and it would be done on his turf.

She asked me to contact him and see if he would be a guest, too. By the time I got out of there I was obsessed all over again. I was ready to convince my father to join me. I didn't mention a word to anybody about it, not even my family, until I spoke with my father. I was afraid they'd try to talk me out of it and I wasn't going through what I went through last time. It was like a circus after the Stern show. I was confident that Geraldo would handle things differently and not allow anything to get out of hand. Besides, this time around it would only be about our relationship.

When I called my father I was very honest and filled him in as much as I knew about the show. I told him there would be a family counselor present and other guests who were kids of famous fathers. He sounded leery and asked me a million questions. That's when I gave him the producer's number and told him that he needed to call her so that he could discuss the details further. I knew by the time I got in the next day I would have an answer. I hung up the phone and went to sleep with my fingers crossed.

I lay in bed half the night questioning myself. What did I expect to get out of this? Suppose it does more harm than good, or backfires on me? Could this really accomplish something? Am I crazy enough to believe that this might make me a star, or better yet a son? Will he listen to me this time and really hear me? Maybe one of the counselors will get him to apologize. I should only be so lucky to have that happen on television. I'm just praying that he doesn't act like a jerk or try to talk down to me like he did on the radio. I'll strangle him right on television in front of the whole world if he tries that bullshit. Then the ratings would really go through the roof. I could watch the promos from jail. "Pat Cooper's son strangles his father on the next Geraldo."

I don't know why I was driving myself crazy that night doing all that projecting when I really believed in my heart that he wasn't going to show up anyway. There was nothing I wanted more than for this to happen. It took me my whole life to finally confront him and I knew I might never get the chance or have the balls to do it again.

When I got in the next day the producer told me it was a go. I was so overjoyed that I kissed her. We would be taping a couple of weeks after the New Year and she said the airdate was usually a week after that. She told me that my father couldn't physically make it to the taping because of a previous commitment, but that he would be there via telephone. I was disappointed and I think she was too. For some reason I didn't buy the story he gave her. I had my heart set on confronting him face to face and now he was going to hide behind the telephone. So typical of him!

When I got to the florist that afternoon I was still excited. I called up everyone screaming, "I'm gonna be on TV! I'm gonna be on TV!" My mother couldn't believe it even though I always said to her; "I'd have my day in court." When Bill found out he was shocked. I told him it was destiny all over again, and thanked him because none of this would have happened if it hadn't been for his wake-up call.

In the days leading up to the taping, I kept busy writing down my thoughts and ideas for the show. That was a challenge in and of itself because I had a lot to say and only a short time to say it. The producer told me from the start that I wouldn't be getting more than a few minutes to tell my story or make a point. She gave me a lot of homework to do that week, but the end result was an accomplished opening statement.

On the day we taped the show I took off from work and brought my cousin Judy along for support. I felt anxious and a bit paranoid that something would go wrong at the last minute. After fifteen minutes of running around the studio like a chicken without a head, they sent me into makeup. By the time I got out of there we were ready to begin.

I took my designated seat and within minutes big bright lights flooded the stage. Once the audience began applauding, I knew Geraldo had entered the room. It was show time. He welcomed everybody and opened with a brief introduction. After showing a video clip and explaining the focus of the show, he introduced all the guests, including my father. All of a sudden I felt important. I was not only an intern on the show, but now only two and a half months later I was a guest.

It was a dream come true and now it was my turn to be heard. This time he had to listen. It took me thirty-two years to get here and less than a minute to tell him what was on my mind. My opening statement challenged him as a father and caught him by surprise. I hesitated for just a split second and then the words came pouring out of my mouth.

"My father's whole act is based on his family. He portrays the image that he's close to me, both mentally and emotionally. The truth about my father is that he's never been there as a father nor has he represented any kind of role model to me in the past thirty years. Pat Cooper's image is a lie that he sold to the American public by turning his back on his own flesh and blood. And that's the true story about him that's been going on for thirty years. I have tried many times to get close to him."

Before I could finish the sentence Geraldo interrupted and asked my father to respond. He immediately got defensive and started with the same Pat Cooper script that he used on the radio, except this time it wasn't working. That made him crazier and more erratic. I couldn't see through the phone wires but I was sure his eyeballs were popping out of his head. Within minutes he started belittling me. He said that I wasn't worth being his son and screamed repeatedly that he didn't want to be my father. That's when I cringed and felt like lunging at him. So that's what he's been trying to tell me all these years, I thought. He really doesn't want to be my father. That has always been my biggest fear and the reality was hard to swallow. He really doesn't want to have anything to do with me. That was the bottom line. Why did he wait so long to tell me? I felt like running off the stage and crying in a corner somewhere, but I knew that's what he wanted. I would have never given him the satisfaction of losing my composure especially on television. I'll never forget the look on the faces in the audience after that. Even when Geraldo demanded that he stop, he continued to scream his head off. That was the moment if he was sitting next to me that I would have killed him.

After the first commercial break Geraldo took some questions and comments from people in the audience. All three of them were repulsed by my father's attitude and tone of voice. When given a chance to respond he continued to cry victim and insinuated, once again, that my mother was the reason for him not being able to be a father to me. That infuriated me even more. It was such bullshit and he held on to that lame excuse as far back as I could remember. When I was a kid my grandmother used to take me to see him all the time and he knew that. My mother never said a word about it. Even if she did, then what was his excuse when I got older? I've been chasing him my whole life and all I ever got was the cold shoulder. He was the one that wasn't interested and showed that just by what he said to me five minutes ago. He always put me off and now everybody knew. He was the living proof that fatherhood cannot be forced.

Last, but not least, the family counselor spoke. I was most interested in hearing her take on this and hoping she could fix things or at least point us in the right direction. I knew this was the closest that I would ever get to real therapy with my father. She didn't offer me much of a solution, but made an assessment about him that helped me to see things more clearly. Her final thoughts were sympathetic and she told me it was time to forget about him and move on with my life.

When we came back from the break Geraldo moved on to the next guest. I was so beside myself that I have no recollection of what happened after that. It was as if I left the stage or had an out-of-body experience. I sat there mortified and thinking about the hurtful shit he just said to me in front of all those people, knowing that in a week when the show aired, the whole country would find out what a jerk he was. He clearly denied his fatherhood and put me down in front of America. Everything he said that day hurt. I believe that was his intention and it was the aftershock of those comments that really got to me the most.

In the final moments of the show Geraldo gave us the chance to make a couple of quick closing statements. My father went first. He addressed two people on the panel but made no mention of a solution or a future plan. He left off on a sour note when he arrogantly reminded Geraldo that Pat Cooper was the only celebrity that showed up. I in turn commented that I tried loving my father and concluded that it might be too late to work things out. As soon as I started to say more, Geraldo gave me the signal that the time was up.

Pat Cooper did show up that day. He was right about that, but I was expecting my father, Pasquale Caputo. Why did I believe the confrontation on television would make him show up? Nothing was accomplished that day except a little self-satisfaction of finally standing up to him. Unfortunately, he walked away with more ammunition and new material under his belt. I ended up hurt. That was the price I had to pay for confronting him and the reason why I was so afraid to do it all those years. Here was a sixty-year old man who continuously ignored me and went around thinking it was okay. He treated me like damaged goods and made me feel like a pain in the ass all the time. What else in God's name would it take to break through that wall and find out who he really is? I walked off that stage devastated.

It was time to leave and I couldn't wait to get out of there. After checking on my cousin and sending her home, I ran backstage to get my things. I thought that was the time I might hear some feedback. I was surprised that nobody said a word. But after seeing some of their faces, I understood why. When Geraldo saw me he invited me into his dressing room and offered me a beer. He said that I needed one and we both kind of laughed. He commented that I handled myself exceptionally well considering the circumstances. That was the first time I officially met my boss and his opinion meant a lot to me. We spoke only for a few minutes and before I left I felt much better. I was just about to walk out the door when he reminded me to take off my makeup. I hated wearing that stuff and suddenly had a flashback of the time when my grandmother and her sisters dressed me up like a girl. I don't know why that came back to haunt me, in Geraldo's dressing room no less, but I remember the day my aunts piled it on my face just as thick. That's all I needed now was to roam around the neighborhood looking like that. I had enough humiliation for one day.

In the halls I met up with some of the people from the audience. Most of them just stared at me, but a few of them stopped and wished me good luck. One woman even asked me for an autograph and made me feel like a celebrity. After signing her notepad, "Michael Caputo— Pat Cooper's son," I flew down the stairs and ran all the way home.

When I walked in the door I was still so overcharged from everything. It took a couple of days to come down, and discussing it on the phone all weekend just prolonged it. It wasn't until Sunday night that I really had the chance to digest it all. I knew I hadn't heard the last of my father and had a strong feeling that he would be on the radio first thing in the morning crying to Howard Stern about the Geraldo show. In fact, there was no way in the world he wouldn't be there, only this time I had plans to be there, too. He wasn't getting away with what he said to me on television. This time he'll get the chance to tell me to my face that he doesn't want to be my father. Then I'm really going to let him have it. I'll fix his ass good this time even if it means lowering myself to his level. We'll have our first father and son "talk" right on the Howard Stern show where it all started. When I'm done in that studio he'll remember I'm his son. I'm tired of being ignored. It's time the stand-up comic becomes the stand-up dad and apologizes.

The first couple of days after the taping there was nothing on Howard Stern about my father not even a mention of his name. That was the calm before the storm. By Wednesday morning all that changed. As soon as I heard them say Geraldo and Pat Cooper in the same sentence, I hopped into a cab and flew crosstown to Madison Avenue. On the way over I made the cabdriver put on the Stern show. I didn't want to miss anything and I knew my father was about to go on the air at any minute. By seven-fifteen I was standing in the lobby of Infinity Broadcasting, home of 92 K-Rock.

I had a panic attack on the way up in the elevator wondering if they were going to let me in or not. When the doors opened I approached a man who I assumed worked there. I told him who I was and said I wanted to join my father in the studio. He immediately introduced himself as Gary the producer. After our little conversation he went inside to inform Howard. I sat there on the couch for almost fifteen minutes listening to the show that was being played from an overhead speaker. My father was already giving his version of what happened on the Geraldo show. It was just like I thought; only now he was telling everybody that I set him up. The more he spoke the more my blood boiled. In the middle of all that Stern announced that I was waiting in the lobby. I heard him ask my father, more than once, if it was okay to let me into the studio. Once he got his approval the producer returned and escorted me in.

We took about ten steps and then he sat me in front of a huge console. Howard was sitting on his throne about fifteen feet to my left and Robin was in a booth all by herself to my far right. My father was sitting about twenty feet directly across the way from me. Because of the size of the room and all the equipment I couldn't get a complete view of his face, but I could see he was pissed.

They welcomed me, and then we got right down to business. I felt on the defensive right from the start because of what I previously heard in the lobby. It took a while to explain my side of the story because Stern kept interrupting me, either to joke or to ask questions. In the process my father threw in his two cents, but Stern still managed to keep everything calm and conversational. It was during this time that I plugged the airdate of the Geraldo show, which happened to be my sister's birthday (January 19). Was that fate taking control again or just another coincidence? It took me more than half the show to make my point—that there were two sides to the story: Pat Cooper's version and the truth. The overall opinion in the room was that I sabotaged a relationship with my father and set him up on the Geraldo show. We argued that for a while and then got off on another issue. My father's beef was that I went on national television and accused him of abandonment. I quickly corrected him and explained that the theme of the show was about fatherhood, in general, and that I never even mentioned the word abandonment. I reminded him that my opening statement that day only referred to his emotional responsibilities as a father and nothing else. In plain English I said he was never there for me. When he tried to blame my mother again, that's when I exploded. "My mother was there! My mother was there! Where were you?" I screamed.

"Your mother had to be there! She had to be there!" He screamed.

"What do you mean she had to be there? You had to be there, too!"

"She's your mother. She's your mother. She had to be there!"

"Where were you for thirty years? Where were you the last thirty years?"

"I was in America. I was in America," he said trying to make a joke out of it.

"Answer it! Answer it!" I demanded in a serious tone.

"I was in America."

"Yeah, how come the phones weren't ringing?"

"I didn't want to call ya! I don't want to call ya!" He repeatedly screamed.

"That's right. You didn't want to call. That's the bottom line!"

"I don't want to call anyone who talks the way you talk!"

"That's the bottom line. That's the bottom line," I concluded.

"That's right! It's over, baby, so you can forget about it! He screamed.

After the first blowup the conversation switched back to the Geraldo show again and the abandonment issue. Howard and Robin were making a few points and trying to establish some peace. That's when my father interrupted and stated his own solution.

"I'll solve the problem right now. It ends here. You got my word as a man; it ends here with him and me. I won't bother with him no more. I won't call him," he said spitefully.

"Wait a second. Can I say something? Can I say something? All my life, all my life…" I pleaded.

[Everybody was talking at the same time and I was trying to get my point across. There was chaos in the room and I was only seconds away from blowing up again.]

179

"All my life, all my life, Robin, my father has found an excuse not to bother with me. Now he's got another reason...okay, this is another reason. Now he's got a good reason this time." I said

"He can kiss my butt! This is the end of it as of now. He can kiss my butt! Now he can tell the world that I abandoned him, cause I'm abandoning him now!" He screamed

"The world knows you were a fake for thirty years. You were a fake! You were never a father to me!" I said repeatedly.

"A fake? Look at this! You wish you had a father like me!" He screamed.

"Wish? Who wishes? Who wishes? I asked loudly and repeatedly.

[At that point Robin intervened and it was a good thing because I wouldn't have stopped. She suggested a way that we could work things out, but my father already had his mind made up.]

"It's never gonna work, Robin, because I ain't gonna let it work. It's over! That's the end of it! I'm saying it publicly so you got it on record," he said.

"I'm glad everybody heard. This is what I heard for thirty years."

"You never heard it for thirty years."

"That's what he always says, his favorite line, 'You blew a father, you blew a father, you blew a father!'" I said mockingly.

"Goodbye, goodbye," he screamed repeatedly.

[At this point he was trying to drown me out and intimidate me again. But I came back even stronger.]

"Like it was my fault, he put me here, now he turns his back on me!"

"Goodbye, goodbye! He didn't hear me. I'll say it again," he screamed louder.

"Goodbye, goodbye to you!" I said, upstaging him.

"Goodbye! That's all!"

"Goodbye to you! Go back to Vegas in your little bubble out

there." I said sarcastically.

"I'll go where I want to go."

"Go back to Vegas with your little make-believe family."

"Oh now I'm make-believe."

"Yeah, the Pat Cooper make-believe family! Go back to Vegas!"

"Now you're knocking my wife and my daughter. They got nothing to do with this."

"Like you never knocked us...That's all I ever heard for thirty years!" I snapped back at him faster than a bullet.

"My wife and my daughter never knocked yous."

"You knocked my mother and my grandmother and my sister for thirty years. You're the vindictive one! You're vindictive!" I screamed.

"All right, Mike, all right, its over," he said.

[I continued driving my point.]

"You're the one who knocks the family all the time. Your own mother you even knocked!"

"I don't knock, I defend! There's a difference!" He snapped.

"You knocked your own mother! You want respect, but you knock your own mother!" I screamed.

"That's right! That's right, because my mother wasn't a mother!"

"What do you mean she wasn't a mother?"

"That's right. You don't like it? Too bad! I'll knock who I want!" He screamed.

"Then I'll knock who I want to knock. And if that means my father, then it means my father, because you're wrong! You're out of line!"

"Good, cause then it's over. You're out of line."

"No, you're out of line, Dad. You're out of line!" I insisted.

"All right so we're both out of line."

[After his conclusion Howard and Robin burst out laughing. There was a slight pause, but I kept going.]

"He wants respect, but he doesn't know how to give respect. You got to learn how to give it before you can get it," I said.

"You all wouldn't know respect if it hit you over the head with a bat!" He shouted.

"Yeah, look whose talking. Look whose talking, Pat Cooper!" I snapped.

[After arguing on and off for forty minutes nothing was accomplished. I sat there emotionally drained and waiting for Howard or Robin to say something. But my father beat them to it and dropped the bomb on me again. Howard sensed something big was coming and so did I. He tried to rush to a commercial, but my father insisted on making a statement first.]

"Can I tell you something, Howard? I'm glad this happened because I'm going back to my make-believe world. I don't want to be a part of his world. I'm telling you right now that I don't want to be his father and that's the way it's gonna be!"

"I'm glad he said it on the air," I announced. "Everybody heard that! He doesn't want to be my father. Pat Cooper is no longer Michael Caputo's father!"

"Absolutely, now I tell you that's the truth and you got it on tape," he affirmed.

[He said it again, only now he rubbed it in my face. I thought I'd be ready for it this time—I wasn't. I was never ready for it and I couldn't take the rejection anymore. Now I know what my grandmother meant when she said to him, "It would have been better if you stabbed me!"]

Those remaining minutes on the air left me quite disturbed. Howard saw that and came up with something real quick. After taking a few phone calls and a vote, the unanimous decision was to give us another try. But that's what everybody else wanted. Nobody even asked me what I wanted or how I felt. There was nothing more to try for. This was not a callback. I already got the part thirty-two years ago. I'm not auditioning to be his son; I am his son. God damn it! Was I supposed to try to be a better victim? Is that what they wanted? What was in it for me, or is it only about the ratings? That little voice inside me told me that the next time would be nothing more than a rerun. Before I could give Stern an answer he suggested a six-week hiatus and an open invitation to return. Even though my father agreed, every muscle and bone in my body told me that he was never going back into that studio, at least not with me there.

I left there feeling worse than I did after the Geraldo taping. It was sickening. Even after confronting my father face to face nothing got accomplished. And now I had to wait another six weeks to try again. For what? When did I get on this roller coaster and how many more rides would it take before I can finally get off? It's hard to believe he's from the same family and found success in all that rage.

After the Geraldo show aired people treated me differently. Suddenly, there was a certain respect and acknowledgment that I had achieved just by going on television with this. The feedback was more intense and positive than when I had gone on the radio. I had touched people's lives in a way that I never thought possible. Within a week there were letters sent from all over the country with all kinds of advice and encouragement not to give up. Even though I was grateful, I remained deeply frustrated.

My family was more supportive this time around, which made me feel good. They had finally accepted the fact that I was going to deal with my father the way I wanted to. The bottom line was that they just didn't want to see me get hurt again.

I spent the majority of the weekend celebrating my television debut back in the old neighborhood with my friends. The topic of conversation was my father and I, and everyone had something to say. By the time I got home Sunday night I had Pat Cooper and the Geraldo show coming out of my ears. And I still had to get up at six o'clock in the morning to hear Howard Stern's reaction.

To my surprise everything died down much faster this time around. Stern only made a few comments on Monday morning and then the rest of the week it was like nothing ever happened. I prayed it wouldn't be a mistake going back into that studio. Maybe everybody was right and it would be worth another try, but I made up my mind that the next one was going to be my last one. I knew that in six weeks I'd be ready to give my father another chance. Hopefully, by then he would have come to his senses. If not, it was the end of the ride. In the meantime I kept listening to the show in case there were any changes.

One morning, just two weeks later, I got the surprise of my life. At first I thought Stern was playing excerpts from a previous show. But when I heard my father comparing me to "Judas" and saying that I betrayed him, I knew what I was hearing was live. That's when I went berserk. I grabbed the telephone with such force that I almost broke one of my fingers. I couldn't even dial the number because I was so nervous. Then I kept getting a busy signal. Even when the operator tried for me I couldn't get through. That made me even crazier. Why hadn't they kept their promise? What happened to the six-week hiatus? Why didn't they call me? What the hell is my father doing on the radio bad mouthing me again? Since when did Stern and my father become best friends? I had an open invitation, too, and I distinctly remember them telling me that. Without thinking any further, I grabbed my jacket and flew out the door. I was livid and determined to put an end to this bullshit once and for all.

On the way over to the radio station all I kept thinking about was getting there before my father left. The cab driver was making good time, but when we hit traffic on 57th Street I got out and ran the rest of the way. Even though it was cold out, by the time I got to 60th Street I was sweating profusely. I forgot all about that as soon as I stepped off the elevator and heard my father's voice. He was still on the air carrying on. That's when I headed straight toward the studio, only this time Gary the producer wouldn't let me in. For a few seconds I tried to force my way in by pushing my body weight against the door. Gary was doing the same thing on the other side and trying to prevent things from getting ugly. I wasn't about to stop, but he calmly and quickly diffused the situation when he politely said, "You can't do this, Mike. We can't let you in here. It's your father who doesn't want you here, not us. He threatened to leave the studio if we let you in this time." When the truth hit me it felt like all the blood completely drained out of my body. I immediately backed off and responded, "Don't worry, Gary, I'm not gonna make any trouble here. I'm not crazy like him." At first it didn't look like he believed me, but after I apologized a couple of times he finally let go of the door. I felt embarrassed and quickly left the building.

I waited for my father outside in the cold for fifteen long minutes. When he exited the building he looked like Bozo the clown. He had made his hair lighter and I thought to myself; with all his money he couldn't even get himself a decent dye job. It was so orange looking and it stood out even more against his long black cashmere coat. He noticed that I was waiting by the curb and made believe he didn't see me. He started walking south on Madison Avenue. I ran behind him and shouted, "What's your problem, Dad?" He ignored me and kept on walking. That's when I jumped in front of him, this time cutting him off. "What's the matter? I repeated. You have nothing to say now?"

"I don't want to talk, it's over," he said. Then he made an about-face and began walking uptown. Every time I opened my mouth to say something he would turn away from me and walk in the opposite direction. The more he did that the more I put myself in his face. He was just about to cross the street when he startled me by coming to a sudden stop. "I'm such a terrible person, Mike, aren't I? Maybe you want to push me in front of the cars, too?" I couldn't believe he said that. My father had come up with some winners in his life, but that was by far the most pathetic.

"No I don't want to throw you in the middle of street," I responded. "I want some fuckin answers and I want them now!" We were only three feet apart and he still wasn't making eye contact with me.

"I have nothing to say. We're through and I just feel bad for you because you blew a father," he said, looking down at the ground.

"Blew a father, blew a father, I never had a fuckin father," I screamed looking directly into his face. "That's the problem. Where were you the last thirty years? Tell me that!"

"I was right here, my friend," he quickly responded. At that moment I flipped out on him and wanted to pound his fuckin head into the pavement for calling me his friend.

"You're full of shit! You're full of shit!" I screamed. "You were never here, never!" That's when he started to walk away again. I didn't run after him this time, instead I yelled loud enough so he could hear me all the way down the block.

"Go ahead, walk away! Walk away, Pat Cooper! That's what you did for the last thirty years! For thirty years you walked away from me!" That's when I noticed that people passing by were staring at me. They were hurrying by me, too. Either they were cold, in a rush, or thought that I was a lunatic and were trying to avoid me. Maybe it was all three. I singled out one woman and spoke to her as I pointed down the block at my father. "See that man walking down the street…that's the comedian Pat Cooper. He's my father. He walked away from me just like that thirty years ago." She gave me a weird look and just kept on moving.

Suddenly, my heart felt as cold as the outside air and I began shivering uncontrollably. I had never felt so alone in my life. I ran away from that block hating him and despising every bone in his body. I knew I had to get on with my life and that meant letting go. There was no other way and I had to start now. But would I be able to after all those years of hanging on? How do I let go when every time I look in the mirror I see his face? How do I let go when someone or something always brings me back to him? Even when I step into an Italian restaurant I stand the chance of seeing his picture hanging on the wall. How, when every time I tell a joke I hear his voice? How do I let go of blood? How, when I still believe in my heart that there was something more I could have done? I wondered how much longer it would take me to come to terms with this.

It took a few weeks to get over the scene I had with my father on Madison Avenue. That being said, I never really got over it; I just managed to stop dwelling on it twenty-four seven. That was only half the battle. I never told my friends or anybody in the family what happened that day. In fact, I never called my father or listened to him on the Howard Stern show ever again. I even told my friend Bill not to mention when my father was on. It was the only way I knew how to move forward and begin to heal.

Things at the Geraldo show changed and it couldn't have come at a better time. It was an unexpected surprise when they moved out of the Times Square studio and into the CBS studios on West 57th Street. Over there I was exposed to the taping of the Joan Rivers show and that presented new opportunities. I made it a point to go in extra early every morning so I could work on her show, too. It was at her office where I met a promotions producer who took me under his wing. Working with Tom and being his personal assistant was the best thing that could have happened to me. I knew this would be my chance to prove myself and finally get hired.

My usual pastime at CBS was hanging out in the control room and working with some of the high-tech equipment. One of the directors turned me on to an incredible photo machine and it was love at first sight. It allowed me to take pictures during the actual taping of the Joan Rivers show while simultaneously printing out the results. That fascinated me and I parked myself in front of that machine as much as I could, especially when I knew that one of my favorite celebrities would be on. That's when I would click away like a crazy man capturing the highlights of the show. And the best part was after I was done using the photographs for my work, I got to keep them as souvenirs.

One morning during the first week of May I found out at that Angela Bowie and Howard Stern would be coming in to do the show. I thought they would be terrific guests and great for the ratings, but I worried that seeing Stern again would bring back too many sour memories of my father. I was just beginning to put all that behind me and I didn't want to have any setbacks. Besides, I still felt ashamed for trying to force my way into his studio the last time I was there. Stern probably forgot all about it the minute I left, but for me it was still very fresh in my mind.

All eyes and ears were on Angela Bowie that morning and for good reason. She had some gossip about her ex-husband David Bowie that she wanted to make public on the Joan Rivers show. Nobody knew for certain what she would say, but we all knew it was going to be something juicy. At first she wasn't very forthcoming with the dirt and that kept the studio audience in suspense. I think she did that purposely. Even Joan was on the edge of her seat trying to pull it out of her. It wasn't until Stern was added to the mix that Angela finally delivered the goods. After some coaxing from him she blurted out that she once caught her ex in bed with rocker Mick Jagger. While everybody was in a state of shock, I snapped a picture and captured that scandalous moment forever. It was a beautiful color shot of Stern sitting between Joan Rivers and Angela Bowie with his arms wrapped around the both of them. I was very proud of that picture and wanted to do something more than just stick it in the desk with the rest of my collection. That's when my boss hinted that it would impress the VIP's and be good for the show if I ran the photo over to the Daily News that day. That's all I had to hear. I didn't promise him anything, but I managed to get the picture over there on my way down to the flower shop. When I got into work it was so busy that I totally forgot to call Tom and let him know that I made it there.

The next morning at CBS they treated me like a hero. Tom came running over to me with all smiles, thanking me a hundred times for dropping the picture off. I thought he was over-reacting until he told me that it was front-page news. When he showed me a copy of the papers, I almost dropped dead. The headlines read "Dancing in the Sheets?" Below that was a picture of rock icons David Bowie and Mick Jagger with a caption underneath stating what Angela Bowie had said about them on the show. On the second page was the full story with the famous picture that I had taken in the control room the day before. That's when I started jumping up and down like I just hit the lottery.

I got enough attention that day to last me the rest of the year. Even when I got home I received a phone call from one of the top executives in Chicago praising me for a job well done. The following week when I returned to work they hired me. My title: Assistant Promotions Producer for Tribune Entertainment.

Eight months as an intern with persistence and hard work finally paid off. I was able to quit the flower shop for the second and final time, which was the answer to my prayers. It was amazing how just one photograph and a trip to the Daily News had turned my whole life around. It put me on the map at CBS and established me as a serious player. I got a lot of mileage out of that picture, more than I ever expected. It was even in one of the major tabloids two weeks later. There I was standing on line at the neighborhood supermarket with a copy of the Star Magazine staring me in the face bearing that same picture. I smiled and thought to myself; this is what it must feel like to be a famous photojournalist, except no one knew that I was the photographer. I only wish somebody would have told Howard Stern that I was the one who got his picture in the paper. In some funny way I felt like I had returned the favor for all the time and publicity he gave me. Too bad I never got the chance to tell him.

By the end of the summer I was having second thoughts about working in television. I was on my way to becoming a producer someday, but my heart just wasn't into it anymore. It was only a few months earlier that I would have done anything to work in that industry, but that became less appealing to me as I began to let go of my father.

Chapter Ten

- Praying for Time -

In late September I said goodbye to my short television career. The people at Tribune were shocked and my family thought I was crazy. The same VP that praised me earlier that year called me and tried to convince me to stay. He was very nice and said the door would always be open. When I hung up the phone I started to feel a little sad and couldn't figure out why. Then it hit me. I had no job! What the hell was I thinking walking out of there like that, especially without having something else lined up? I couldn't collect unemployment even if I wanted to. I began to have a panic attack and immediately started calling everyone in the family for help and asking them what I should do. I was hoping, maybe they could give me some advice. If not, I'd have to go back to the flower shop. And that was the last thing I wanted to do. I didn't care if I had to sweep floors for a living; I wasn't going back there.

Why did I keep sabotaging myself? This time I had a good job. I was living in Manhattan and I couldn't afford to be out of work, not even for a day. I did the same thing right before I left for California. I gave up everything I loved and ran away from everyone. My head was all fucked up again and all because of Pat Cooper. I allowed myself to get caught up with the anger and the lingering resentment. I was trying to let it go, but it was eating me up inside—knowing that my father still had such an affect on me. It was a vicious cycle with no end in sight.

Two days later my cousin got me a job at an upscale perfumery on the east side. This time instead of selling flowers and bouquets I was selling fancy soaps, colognes, and aromatherapy oils. I hated retail and wasn't used to working for minimum wage, but I was in no position to turn it down. In less than two weeks I felt like I was going out of my mind. Thank God it was only part-time. I think I would have killed myself if I had to work there forty hours a week.

One day while I was in the gym a massage therapist approached me and started giving me a speech about the benefits of massage. The next thing I knew I was laying on a padded table being rubbed with warm almond oil. Here was this total stranger rubbing my body and making every muscle feel like jello. I remember thinking to myself: I could do this for a living! This had to be the most appreciated and lucrative job in the world. When I got off the table I was a new man. After picking the therapist's brain I immediately went home and made an appointment to visit a massage school in Manhattan the very next day.

It was another snap decision to go to the Swedish Institute, but this time it seemed right. I had spent years trying to keep my head above water and I felt that this career would finally keep me afloat. I had to do something with my life and I had to decide fast. I thought about it a million times; was this massage idea something I really wanted to do? It felt wonderful getting a massage, but would I enjoy giving them, too? I wasn't really sure, but then I thought fate put this in my face for a reason, just like it had with other things before. I learned to trust destiny and after auditing a class I made up my mind to go. I was still kind of nervous, especially knowing it would be a year commitment and another five years on top of that to pay off my student loan. My grandmother gave me one of her looks when I told her I was going to another school and my mother was just speechless. My roommate didn't care either way; he already knew he was living with a nut job.

The massage program was intense and at times it felt like medical school. There were three tests a week and more anatomy and physiology than I had ever imagined. It got to be overwhelming at times, but looking at the bright side—I didn't have time to obsess over anything else. It kept my mind occupied which helped me to forget about how angry I was. I knew if I stayed focused and kept a positive attitude, I'd be fine.

The same month I finished school I switched jobs and began working at the front desk at my gym that was owned and run by a chiropractor. I knew that environment would be a major opportunity and a gold mine for potential clients. I loved that job and had the most fun ever. Sometimes it didn't even feel like work. I would open the place at 6 AM sharp and motivate everybody with my disco tapes. I had a blast and never felt like leaving that job. But I knew once I had my license all that fun would end and it would be time to move on to bigger and better things. And that's exactly what I did. It was at the gym that I became friendly with a personal trainer named Ben. He hooked me up with a friend of his who got me my first professional gig working at a five-star hotel spa.

For the next five years life was good. I became an uncle twice and had the honor of being the godfather for one of my nephews. My schedule at work was ideal—five hour shifts and only four days a week. I had more free time on my hands than I knew what to do with. One of the reasons why I got into that business in the first place was to be able to make the most amount of money in the least amount of time. That was all well and good, but after a while I got bored. I needed something else to fill in the gap—something to stimulate me besides the gym. That's when I decided to become a parent. I took a long train ride out to Huntington, Long Island, and bought myself a dog—just like that! He was a purebred, an eight-week old West Highland terrier who I named Casey. It was a choice between him and his two brothers. After watching them play for a while I chose the pup that had the most energy like me. He was also the one out of the litter who wouldn't stop licking my hands. That's all it took to win me over. I snatched him up, threw down six hundred dollars and got his papers.

On the way home I made a promise to him that I was going to be the best father and he would have the greatest life ever. I fell in love with that dog right from the start. I used to show him off and brag to everybody that I had him house broken within a month. I was so fastidious about my apartment even the dog knew. I had heard some real horror stories from other dog owners who lived in the city. There was no way my dog was going to shit all over my house and chew on the furniture while I was at work. I spent hours with him in Central Park and on the days we couldn't make it there—we hung out on the roof of my building playing ball. He was a happy dog and didn't care what we did—as long as we were together. I treated him like a son and even scheduled our haircut appointments on the same day. I found a vet, a trainer, and an animal psychologist who made house calls. Just my luck, Casey needed a shrink, too. He had a weird behavior—regurgitating his food and then eating it up again. I never heard of such a thing and he did that after every single meal. It was beyond gross! Even the psychologist couldn't figure out what the problem was and it ended up costing me three hundred dollars anyway. After I told one of the ladies at the park about my experience she convinced me to take out health insurance for him just in case he had a real issue. When I asked my grandmother what she thought about pet health insurance she told me that I should have my head examined and just give her the money instead.

Being a pet owner was a huge responsibility and more time consuming than I expected, but it was no match for the unconditional love and loyalty I got in return. It was amazing how quickly that dog bonded with me. All in all, getting Casey was one of the best things I ever did.

In the spring I received a call that changed my life. I'll never forget that day. I was standing in the doorway of my bedroom when the telephone rang. I was just about to walk out the door and take the dog to the park. In fact, I had my coat on and he was already on the leash. It was his fifth birthday and we were going to celebrate. When I picked up the phone it was my Aunt Marie—my grandmother's youngest daughter. She sounded subdued and serious. I knew something was up and Aunt Marie—being Aunt Marie got right to the point.

"Hi, how are you doin?" She paused for a couple of seconds then dropped the bomb on me.

"I got bad news. Grandma's got cancer." Suddenly I felt cold like all the blood had left my body. I started shaking uncontrollably and all I could hear were the words cancer and grandma echoing in my head. I even thought the dog could hear it.

"Grandma's had this chronic cough for a while now and we had it checked out. They think its lung cancer!" And before she could say anything more I shouted back at her in disbelief.

"Lung cancer—grandma never smoked! Where did that come from—all of a sudden? Are you sure? Does grandma know? Maybe that doctor is wrong, Aunt Marie." Suddenly my head was filled with a million questions.

"We're going to see the doctor—to get the results of the x-rays. It doesn't look too good." she said. "We need you to stay with her a few hours at the house after her appointment."
"Anything...sure...what day is the appointment?" I asked.
"It's tomorrow around three, are you off?" she asked.
"Yeah, no problem, I'll be there, definitely!"
"Michael, listen, don't say anything to grandma about the cancer. She doesn't know and we want to make sure first."
"Sure, sure...no...I won't say a word, I promise!"

When I got off the phone I was so depressed that I didn't even feel like going to the park anymore. All I wanted to do was cry and think. Did this mean she was going to die? My grandmother was the only person who had been there for me, besides my mother. She was the one who taught me and encouraged me to love my father despite the circumstances. She had always made me feel special like I was part of something—giving me a sense of self and making me feel whole. She was my heart—my best friend and I couldn't imagine losing her without losing a part of myself. Now what? Did this mean I would have to be the one to tell my father? I wasn't going to say a word to him. It was his mother and he better do the right thing. Maybe this is what he would need to come to his senses—before it was too late. If not, that's his problem. Anyway, I swore I'd never call that fuck again, no matter what.

195

I didn't even want to think about him or his bullshit. It would have only made me angrier and it was too premature to start jumping to conclusions. I had more important things to worry about now. My grandmother was sick and she was number one—not him. I'd deal with my father when the time comes or I'd just let fate take care of him like it always had. Until then I would say my prayers and hope for the best.

I didn't know what to expect when I got to my grandmother's house the next day, I was just anxious to see her. When I first arrived she looked preoccupied, but other than that she seemed like her normal self. It wasn't until we sat down to eat that she started to complain about her health. The word cancer never came up, but I knew just by the look on her face what the results were. She said her cough got so bad at night that it felt like she was choking to death. The doctor had to prescribe strong medication and that made her uneasy. She didn't believe in taking drugs everyday and felt that; although they might cure one thing—they would still upset another. From day one we kept a watchful eye and constantly had to remind her to take those pills.

By the end of the month I was already going to my grandmother's house three to four times a week to pitch in and help take care of her. It became routine and a priority of mine to keep her in good spirits. I really thought, at the onset of everything, that some tender loving care and the right medication would beat the disease. There was no way that a stupid cough could bring my grandmother down. She was too strong and a hell of a fighter. Without realizing it, I was in denial.

Over the summer things got a little better. There were signs that my grandmother's health was improving and at times I even forgot she was sick. She had a good appetite and carried on at the dinner table with her funny stories just like she used to. Every weekend she had a full house and she was in her glory. Then out of nowhere she started getting progressively worse. She lost her appetite, started skipping meals, and didn't even bother to cook. That was not like her. It wasn't too long ago that she used to be able to put away a half a pound of macaroni all by herself. Now she was having trouble swallowing even when she was in the mood to eat. I could see her frustration and I was scared for her. My aunts had to get a couple of nurses to come in and take care of her, which was another nightmare. My grandmother wasn't crazy about any of them. She hated having strangers in the house, especially ones that were unfriendly and couldn't cook. Where the hell did these nurses come from and how could they even call themselves caretakers? I almost threw up when I caught one of them feeding her canned food like she was a cat or something. How did they expect my grandmother to get better with that shit? That's when I decided to buy the food myself, cook it at my house and then bring it over to hers. I'll never forget my grandmother's reaction when I walked in the door with all those plastic containers filled with enough food to last her a whole week. It gave her a good laugh and reminded her of the days when she used to do the same thing for me. But changing the menu was only half the battle—and the easiest part. The real work came when we sat down to eat. I tried coaching her, cutting her food into tiny pieces, and I even tried spoon-feeding her. But nothing worked. There were times when she just sat there staring at the food on her plate. It was so depressing I would run in the bathroom and cry.

One day I called my Aunt Carol just to vent. That was another phone call I'll never forget. I carried on for more than ten minutes about the useless nurses, my grandmother's bad appetite and the side effects of her medication. I didn't let my aunt get a word in edgewise. She called out my name numerous times trying to get my attention, but I just continued on with my monologue as if I didn't hear her. Finally, after the fifth try she succeeded and what she said stopped my motor mouth instantly.

"Michael...grandma's dying! I don't know if you realize that. There's nothing more you could do or any of us could do except continue to be there for her."

Suddenly I had this hollow feeling in the pit of my stomach. I felt so helpless, alone and angry all at the same time. We spoke for another five minutes then I had to get off the phone. I took a couple of long deep breaths and remembered what my grandmother always said to me about talking to God whenever I got upset. This time I didn't talk to him—I begged him. He probably got tired of listening to me that day, but I didn't want to lose my grandmother. I wanted her to live to be a hundred. I never thought the time would come when I'd have to let go of her. And I always had trouble letting go of everything! It took me almost forty years to let go of my father and he only gave me a few crumbs. My grandmother had given me endless memories and years of unconditional love. There could never be enough time on earth for me to let go of that.

That week I finally got to spend some quiet time with my grandmother. It was a rarity in those days with all the company and the twenty-four hour homecare she had. But this particular day was different. The nurse fell asleep in the living room and it was only my grandmother and I at the dining room table. I loved it when I had her all to myself like that. It felt a little strange eating in silence, but neither one of us were in a talkative mood that day. The dripping sound of the kitchen sink made me crazy. It gave me such an eerie feeling. It was as if it was counting the seconds away—reminding me that time was running out.

My grandmother started fussing with her food and eating with her hands which had become routine by then. She looked terrible—drawn in the face and her skin as pale as the dish she was eating from. She hadn't combed her hair or soaked her feet in days. It was obvious that she had lost weight and even more obvious that she was getting weaker. Here was my grandmother, once a vibrant woman with an unquenchable zest for life, now a listless soul holding on to a mere existence. I watched her for a few seconds and tried not to stare. Then the telephone conversation I had had with my Aunt Carol the day before kept popping into my head. Suddenly tears filled my eyes. I looked away and quickly tilted my head down so that my grandmother wouldn't notice. But it was too late—she already caught me. I was about to say something but before the words came out I felt her hand reach from under the table and gently grab mine. Once again tears were coming, only this time they were dripping down my face like that leaky faucet. Seeing that, she kind of half-smiled and squeezed my hand with a firmer touch as if to say: Everything is gonna be all right.

I'll never forget that day. In fact, it still brings tears to my eyes whenever I think about it. While wrestling with the inevitable she allowed me to be myself and infused my spirit with comfort and strength. Through her courage she taught me to accept life, and that gave me a sense of peace that I never felt before. Then to top it off, when I was halfway home I realized she had stuffed two twenty dollar bills in one of my coat pockets. That's the way she was—always looking out for me, even when she was going through hell. For months she had been trying to pay me for all the cooking and food shopping I did for her. But I would never take a dime from her and she knew that. At some point during the day she snuck that money in my coat. As soon as I got in the door I called her and confronted her about it, but she insisted that I keep it. Even though I felt guilty, I let her win this time.

For the next couple of weeks my grandmother and I had some good talks at that dining room table and we did a lot of reminiscing. That was her favorite pastime—telling me stories about my father and evoking sentimental memories of my childhood. She always made me leave that house feeling so good—so special, and those intimate moments we shared are the ones I miss the most.

But things changed after she got sick. It still was great being in her company, but when I left her house I felt terribly sad. I knew her days were numbered and so were my visits. Once something happened to her, the house and everything in it would be sold and gone forever. I hated being morbid, but that was the reality. There would be no more elaborate dinners, no more heart-to-heart talks, and no more get-togethers. There would be nothing left but an empty brownstone and an address. That's when I came up with the idea to videotape her house and everything in it—to create a visual souvenir for myself that I could hold onto and cherish forever. Then whenever I watched that tape I'd be able to go back to that comfortable and secure place I once called home.

I thought the weekend would never come. Saturday was a busy day at work and I couldn't wait for my shift to be over. It seemed like everybody in Manhattan wanted a massage that morning. All I kept thinking about was getting to Brooklyn and making my video. I loved doing all that creative stuff and anything to do with my grandmother or her house simply thrilled me.

As soon as I was done with my last client I flew out of there. I had to meet my roommate by the entrance of the 53rd Street train station and I was already ten minutes late. He was the only one I knew with a camcorder and the only one with the patience to hang out with me all day while I did this thing. My plan was to start videotaping as soon as I got off the F train, which would be at the 7th Avenue stop in Park Slope, Brooklyn. I just had to get some footage of that station! That alone would trigger so many memories of my childhood and it would be the perfect opening for the tape. I can't count the number of times I stood on that platform with my family, patiently waiting for the train to come and take us to Coney Island—our second home.

Thinking about the old neighborhood got me all worked up again. I found myself running through the streets dodging in and out of the people like a nut job. At one point I almost tripped and broke my neck. That would have been real pretty—lying in the middle of Fifth Avenue begging someone to call 911. At that moment I looked up and couldn't believe who I saw jauntily walking along Fifth Avenue only a few yards in front of me. It was my fuckin father! I almost died! What the hell was he doing strolling along in midtown like he didn't have a care in the world? Not a single fuckin care in the world and his mother was dying of cancer. I hadn't seen or heard from that man since he walked away from me on Madison Avenue over seven years ago. All of a sudden he pops up out of nowhere—like he fell out of the sky or something. What were the chances of that? He had an apartment downtown in the village and I thought if I ever ran into him, it would be around there. I was shocked! He was the last person I expected to see and I immediately thought to myself: Oh my God, here we go again!

In seconds I was tailing him and debating with myself whether I really wanted to say hello or not. It was amazing how just seeing him could make my stomach turn. I swear if it wasn't for my grandmother being sick I would have just ignored him. Maybe this time I could persuade him to call his mother or better yet, go see her. For God's sake she was dying and I knew he was well aware of that. His cousin kept him well informed. She was at my grandmother's house a couple of times when I was there and she was the only one in the family that he spoke to. There was no question in my mind that my father knew his mother was sick. Thinking about that, I snuck up behind him and nudged his arm. Simultaneously he turned around, and when he realized it was me—he stopped.

"Hey Mike," he blurted out in a surprised tone. He acted like he was happy to see me, but I didn't buy it for a second.

"Hello!" I said, waiting for him to start a conversation. He had nothing to say and he stood there looking at me with that familiar blank expression on his face expecting me to say something first. It was very awkward, as usual. Then he finally spoke up.
"You work around here?" he asked.
"Yes, I work at a hotel on 55th street.
"What do you do?" he asked.
"I'm a therapist."
"Oh, you give therapy." he said.
"Yeah, I do massage therapy."
"You seem pretty strong for it," he said, making a semi-muscular pose. "You're working out a lot I see?"
"Dad, I've been working out for the past twenty years!"

It was sickening that after all this time he still didn't know anything about me or who I was. And those superficial questions of his were the worst. He was never a good actor and judging from his body language it was quite obvious that he was anxious to leave the minute I stopped him. Then, out of the clear blue, he threw a dig.

"How's your family?" he said, stressing the word, "your," like he wasn't related to me.

"How's your family?" I answered with the same tone.

"My family's fine. They're doin well." he said.

"Well your mother's very sick!" I threw it in his face.

"What do you want me to do?" he shrugged.

"What do you mean, what do I want you to do?" I said glaring at him.

"I haven't talked to my mother in years and I'm not a hypocrite to start talking to her now," he said with a slight smugness.

"What are you proud of it?" I snapped.

He stood there completely detached and ignored me. It was like talking to a fuckin wall. I glanced at the Episcopal Church on my left to give me some strength. I was so aggravated already and couldn't even bear to look at him. I noticed that there were several life-sized saints nestled in the alcoves of the building overlooking the entrance of the church. All of them seemed to be staring at me. I remember thinking: I would need all their help and then some just to get this miserable bastard to feel something. What the hell was wrong with him? Even if lightning struck him that day he wouldn't have felt it. Just looking in his eyes I could see he was empty. He had become a shallow and pathetic old man who never grew up. Here was my sixty-eight year old father, about to lose his mother and still too stubborn to make peace with her. He was determined to take that grudge to his grave. I looked up at the saints a second time and begged for a miracle. While all this was going on in my head he was busy looking around like he was waiting for someone to recognize him or ask for an autograph. I was livid, and all I kept thinking about was getting away from him. I didn't want any of that negative energy to rub off on me. I was about to leave, but he beat me to it. He took a few steps then hesitated a second like he forgot something. I thought he was coming back to say goodbye. Instead, he blurted out in front of everyone on Fifth Avenue: "And when she dies don't any of yous call me!"

I thought my insides were going to explode, and then suddenly my body went numb. I felt nearly paralyzed after those ven-
omous words hit my ears. Just because he had no feelings for his
mother or anyone in the family didn't mean that I didn't have any.
He knew how I felt about her and knew how close we were. Just
the fact that he would say something like that proved that he was
rotten to the core. Did he really expect me to go running back to
his mother and repeat that garbage that came out of his mouth?
Did he think I would even bother to mention that I ran into him?
That's what he wanted me to do. Obviously he didn't know me
very well. I was very protective of my grandmother, especially at
that time, and way over him by then. What was he trying to show
me—that he was still miserable and heartless? I knew that twenty
years ago by the reaction I got from him when he called me right
after I got hurt at the Galaxy discotheque. Then he showed it again
by trying to disgrace me on the Geraldo Show. Anyone who heard
him that day knew he was a mess. He's lucky I wasn't a violent
person because I would've have killed him already. I really felt like
jumping on him that day in front of the church right after he made
that comment to me. Maybe the fact that we were standing on
holy ground saved him. I'll never forget those words for as long as
I live. Now I understand why people snap and go berserk even on
their own relatives.

I walked away from that corner with déjà vu. It was the same
disgusting feeling I had the last time we had words on the street.
Only five minutes with that man and I felt like shit. But once I got
to my grandmother's house and pressed record on the camcorder,
I totally forgot about him. Only five minutes with her and I felt like
a million bucks.

Chapter Eleven
- Mama -

My grandmother's ninetieth birthday was a little more than a month away. In spite of her condition my aunts went ahead and made reservations to celebrate her birthday in a quaint little Italian restaurant in the neighborhood. I knew this could possibly be her last and I wanted to give her something sentimental. Flowers always made her feel special. She used to love popping in on me when I worked at the flower shop in the World Trade Center. She knew she could have anything in the store she wanted yet she preferred the pre-made miniature carnation bouquets or the assorted pompom arrangements. And they always had to be stuffed with extra baby's breath and greens. She cracked me up. I could never convince her to take the cymbidium orchids or any of the Holland tulips. That's the way she was but this time I was going to give her something completely different.

I ordered ninety long stem red roses from a flower shop in the West Village. I told the designer to arrange the roses in three separate vases, thirty in each vase, with tons of baby's breath and greens—of course! My Aunt Marie drove me to the florist and we carefully packed the backseat of her Jaguar with three enormous red velvety bouquets that smelled like heaven. Every bud was perfect and I couldn't wait to see the look on my grandmother's face when I paraded them into her house. She was going to kill me for spending all that money, but I didn't care as long as it put a smile on her face.

As we headed west towards the highway we hit traffic. I turned on the radio and sat there looking out the window reminiscing about the good old days and all the fun I used to have hanging out in this neighborhood. For a minute I thought about my father and wondered if he still had an apartment around here. That was another place I never got to see. My thoughts were pleasantly interrupted when "We Are Family" came on the radio. I loved that song and it always put me in a good mood. My aunt turned up the volume and we got into a serious duet by the time we turned the corner. Then suddenly, as I was glancing out the window taking in the sights, I spotted my father, of all people, wandering along in a baseball cap and jeans. I almost didn't recognize him in that attire. He appeared out of nowhere and I thought to myself: This has got to be another omen.

"Aunt Marie, there's my father...pull over!" I blurted out. "Let's sing that song to him—c'mon! Maybe he'll remember we're related!" We both looked at each other and laughed.

"I can't believe it's him," she said in a serious tone. "I'm going to do more than sing a song to him. He's lucky I don't run him over...the bastard!"
"No, no...give me the fuckin wheel!" I said. "Let me do it!"

She edged her way over to the sidewalk as close as possible. I didn't know what to expect from him this time, but when he sees us he'll probably think we're stalking him or something. Impulsively I lowered the window, and in a deep gravelly voice I yelled out his stage name as loud as I could, "Pat Cooper...Pat Cooper!" That got his attention instantaneously and to my surprise he started marching over to the car with a great big smile on his face. For a second he looked just like my grandmother. Could it be that he was happy to see me? That would be a first. The last time I'd seen my father smile like that was when I was a kid and he took me on my first airplane ride. I couldn't figure out why he was in such a good mood. Maybe he had a revelation in the last couple of weeks. There was definitely a reason why we kept running into each other and he must have realized that by now. Time was running out and I had a feeling that this would be my last opportunity to try and get him to make up with his mother. I didn't give a shit about him anymore. He didn't matter. My main concern was my grandmother. I wanted nothing more than to bring those two together before she died. If I managed to get my father over to her house, or better yet come to the party, she would be so happy and it would be the best birthday gift I could ever give her. All the roses in the world couldn't top that.

Then, just as he was about to step off the curb, that great big smile fell off his face quicker than a heartbeat. Without saying a word he turned around and walked away. It was the most bizarre thing. He didn't even get close enough to the car to see who was driving. And even if he did he wouldn't have recognized my aunt anyway; he hadn't seen his sister in over a decade.

"He thought you wanted an autograph," my aunt said as she quickly pulled away. "That's the only reason why he came over to the car in the first place...the jerk!"

For the remainder of the ride to my grandmother's house my mind flooded with thoughts about my father and my family. I thought to myself; that was the third time my father walked away from me. Well, not really. He's been walking away from me my whole life. That was the third time in a physical sense, and I was proud of myself for not letting it have a devastating effect on me like it did so many times before. I remembered how alone I had felt that cold morning on Madison Avenue and what a basket case I was after that. Seven years later and I was still having flashbacks whenever I walked down that street. But I wasn't alone then, and I'm not alone now, either. I always had people in my corner from the very moment I came into this world, yet I put so much emphasis on trying to get my father's love that I took everyone else's for granted.

I knew that even if I would have called out "Dad" instead of his stage name; he would have never come over to the car. I refer to him as Pat Cooper now, just like his fans do—except I'm not a fan anymore. I gave up on him when he walked away from me the first time, and he doesn't deserve to be called Dad, anyway. That title has to be earned. He'll always be my father; I can't change blood, but a Dad—never in a million years. He doesn't have what it takes to be one.

It dawned on me right then and there, that even if he apologized now, it was too late. I don't need a father anymore. I never thought I'd say that, but he had plenty of chances to make things right with me. I needed a father when I was five to teach me how to tie my shoes or to watch cartoons with me. I needed a father when I was seven to teach me how to ride a bicycle. I needed one at ten to play catch with me, teach me how to throw a ball, and show me how to defend myself. I needed a father to teach me how to shave, how to drive, and how to tie a tie. I needed a father just to be there—period.

Then I started to wonder how he acted with his adopted daughter and why he went out and got another kid when he already had two living in Brooklyn that were his flesh and blood. Did he act like a real Dad or was he Pat Cooper with her, too? Would she even know the difference? Did he ever tell her she was adopted? Did he ever tell her about his other family and that he had two kids from a previous wife? He couldn't possibly have kept that a secret; he only spoke about us every night on stage. Didn't she think it was kind of strange that her father spoke fondly about us in his routine and despised us all in real life? What did she think when she heard him knock his whole family on the Howard Stern Show and when he denied me on the Geraldo Show? What kind of a man did she think her father was then? Did he tell her the truth or just shrug it off and say it was all part of "show biz"? Did she ever ask to see pictures of his real children? Did he have any to show her? What about when it was her birthday? Did he give her a gift? Did he make her feel guilty about expecting one? Did he ever tell her that he loved her? Did he ever hug her? How many times did he say he was proud of her? What about when she was old enough to drive? Did he buy her a car or just lend her his Rolls Royce instead? What about when she wanted to go to college? Did she have to apply for financial aid like my sister and I, or did he pay for it? When she got married did he attend the wedding and give her away like he was supposed to do for my sister? Why did she get all the preferential treatment and my sister and I didn't? Is that part of the package deal when you adopt a child? He was more of a father to her than he ever was to us. She got to do things with him that I only dreamed about.

I thought about how many people have told me over the years that I should turn the other cheek and respect him because "he's still your father." People are amazing: always thinking that some one else's problems are so easy to fix. All I know is, while my father went around making everybody laugh I was the one who went to bed crying. I was the one who bragged to all the kids on the block that my father was a "star" and I never once had anything to show for it. And God knows I wasn't looking for a Rolex or a trip to Bermuda. I'm talking about the basics; we were fuckin dirt poor! I didn't realize it at the time—I was too young to understand. But if it wasn't for my grandmother not charging us rent and a few relatives on my mother's side of the family, we really would have been up shit's creek. It was sometime during that same period that my father told his mother to throw us out if we couldn't pay the rent. That's when all the bull shit started and when my father felt that my grandmother took my mother's side. He knew my grandmother would never throw us out of her house. And where were we going anyway on the big forty dollars a week he sent us? We would have had to go on welfare. My mother worked in a factory, cleaned people's homes, and walked their dogs just so my sister and I would have the most memorable Christmases. My grandmother used to sweat her ass off on that sewing machine making coats for us every year—not to mention all the times she fed us. Everybody chipped in and took a piece of my father's job so my sister and I wouldn't notice that we were slighted. And I'm supposed to respect my father!

He never called us on Christmas, Easter, Communion Day, Confirmation Day, or when we graduated. He didn't even call us up on our birthdays. He never called—period! I always ended up calling his house and that was no picnic either. Most of the times his wife screened the calls and half the times she didn't give him the message. God forbid I didn't have a conversation with her or ask her how she was feeling. If and when he returned the call, my father would lecture me till no end saying that it was my mother's fault that I had no manners. What about all the Father's Day cards I sent him that was never acknowledged? I got so frustrated after a few years that I just gave up and started sending them to my grandmother instead.

I thought about how many times I sat there quietly, and listened to my father knock his mother, my mother, and everyone else in the family? I'm supposed to turn my cheek to that! Did they know how insecure that made me feel, and how scared I was to say anything to him because I was afraid he would close the door for good? How many times did I sit there and bite my tongue just listening to him throw the child support issue in my face saying: "The party's over, the party's over—a few more years you'll be twenty-one and the party's over, Mike!" Do they know how many times he tried to make problems between my mother and me? Did they know how embarrassed I was when I heard the dentist tell my mother that the "Coopers" were giving the office a hard time about the bill? Did they know that the only thing he said to me after I got hurt was "you'll have to gum your food next time because I'm not paying?" Did they know how embarrassed I felt when one of my friends asked me, "Why do you need to apply for financial aid? Your father's Pat Cooper!" Do any of these people realize how desperate I must have been to go on the radio and national television to get his attention? Didn't they hear how he humiliated me in front of the world—not to mention in front of my co-workers? And if anybody heard what he said to me on the street about his mother, "And when she dies don't any of yous call me," would they still think I should respect him then? I don't think so! I wish I had a tape recorder hidden in my pocket so when he said stuff like that, I could play it back for everyone; then maybe they'd understand. Why the hell in the world would I want to respect a father like that when all he did was treat me like shit and ignore me my whole life? That's why it burns my ass when strangers come up to me and talk about respect. What about me? Don't I deserve any?

I couldn't believe the sea of memories and emotions that flooded my brain during that ride to my grandmother's house. It never failed! Every time I ran into my father, even if it was just for five minutes, my day was sabotaged. I wish I could erase him out of my head completely or just change the channel. Better yet—delete him like I do with things on my computer.

When we arrived at my grandmother's house the nurse answered the door; it was like it wasn't my grandmother's house anymore. She always answered her own door, usually with a meatball on a fork. My father said that on his albums, and it was true.

"Delivery for Louise Caputo," I cheerfully announced as I made my way into the house. It was so quiet in there; it felt like nobody was home. I remember the good old days when there was such life in that house. It was always jumping! The sound of toasting glasses, the clatter of dishes, pots and pans, and the frequent outbursts of laughter were all gone now.

I made a dramatic entrance into the dining room and placed the roses down on the table right in front of my grandmother. At first she was too awestruck to speak, but when she saw my aunt and the nurse carry in the other two vases she blurted out, "What's all this?" I laughed to myself and immediately responded, "They're all for you gram, Happy Birthday!"

After a couple of minutes I took the bouquets out of her face and moved them onto the console table right behind her. There I lined them up beautifully in front of a huge gold framed mirror that my grandmother had hanging on the wall for decades. Now it looked like there were twice as many roses. That was the whole idea—to add as much life into that room as possible. I got so preoccupied with rearranging everything that I didn't even hear the nurse or my aunt leave. My grandmother and I would have almost two hours alone before my aunt would return and take us to the restaurant to celebrate grandma's birthday. I was looking forward to that all day.

My grandmother didn't say anything about the flowers. In fact she didn't even comment about her birthday or the party. She just sat there looking down at the table with her hands folded. It looked like she was praying. That was not like her and I knew something was wrong. Besides, the silence was killing me and I had to say something. I took one of the rose buds and playfully tapped it on the back of her head. "What's wrong gram...don't you like the flowers?" She slowly turned around and in a choked up voice said, "Nobody's ever done this for me before!" I immediately stopped what I was doing and knelt in front of her. "Gram, you deserve every single rose. There aren't enough of these things in the world that could show you how I feel." She looked at me with such despair that it brought tears to my eyes. I felt so helpless. Without even thinking I rested my head on her knees and said, "There's nothing else I can do, grandma. These are for all the times that I didn't tell you that I love you." She took her hand and gently placed it on my head. In a barely audible voice she said, "Oh yes you have my grandson, you most certainly have!"

When I looked at her again she was smiling. She cocked her head towards the living room and said, "C'mon, let's go inside. I want to show you the dress I'm wearing tonight." For a moment she sounded like her old self, but I dreaded going in there. That's the room that my aunts had turned into a bedroom ever since she got too weak to climb the stairs. It was a sad reminder of just how sick she really was. That towering oxygen tank and the hospital bed in the middle of the floor made me just want to run out of there.

She pulled out a beautiful purple velvet dress that I had never seen before and commented that it was her favorite color. I nudged her and said, "After all these years, now you tell me that purple is your favorite color! I guess I'm gonna have to bring you ninety lavender roses next week, gram." She gave me a look and said, "Never mind, the red ones are just fine!"

While my grandmother was getting ready I went upstairs to look around. I could get lost up there for hours rummaging through all her pictures. I must have looked at them a dozen times and never once got tired of them. My grandmother never had a photo album; she always kept her whole collection in the drawers by the bed. On the mantelpiece were framed pictures of each and every one of us. Alongside them were two small statues: one of the Blessed Mother and the other of Saint Anthony—my grandmother's favorite patron saint. Between the both of them was a small picture of Jesus. That was my grandmother's setup for as far back as I can remember.

Gazing around the room I noticed something had changed since I videotaped the place. It only took me a few seconds to realize that my picture was missing. The eight by ten glossy that I gave to my grandmother in the eighties was gone. I couldn't imagine what she did with it and why she replaced it with my father's picture instead. When I saw that I felt like throwing it out the window, especially after what he'd done in the village that day. But she was still his mother and I knew I had to respect that.

After an hour of fiddling in that drawer with all the photographs, my grandmother called up to me. I was wondering what was taking her so long. It never failed. Whenever I went upstairs to her bedroom to look around she'd always ask me the same question, "What the hell you doin up there?" And I'd always answer, "Nothing, gram," because she knew what I was doing. We played that game for years; it was hysterical! And if I didn't get my ass down there quick enough, she'd be waiting at the bottom of the stairs waving her fist at me, just like she used to do at Coney Island when I wouldn't get out of the water. That's how she was—always reminding me who's boss. And if I remember correctly she had a heavy right hook, too. But that day it was a very different scenario. She gave me free rein of the place and let me stay up there for as long as I wanted to. She was also unusually quiet and I thought for sure she had fallen asleep. Then out of the blue she called out, "Take what you want! Take your father's picture!" It was like she read my mind. I shouted back, "Thanks" and immediately started unfastening the hooks on the back of the frame. When I got his eight by ten glossy out, I found mine right underneath. I almost died! I thought to myself: Why in world would my grandmother do something like that? Why not just buy another frame? It wasn't like she was cheap. Then I realized, knowing her, she probably figured that was the only way she could get us both together. And with the help of Saint Anthony, the Blessed Mother and Jesus, her prayers would eventually be answered.

But why did she put his picture on top of mine? Could it be because it had become warped and faded and she would have felt guilty throwing it out, or was it something deeper than that? It was bothering me so much that I decided to go downstairs and ask her about it. I knew she would have a good explanation, but I still wanted to hear it from her mouth anyway. It wasn't until I got to the bottom of the steps that it dawned on me. Now it all made sense! She saw me not only as her grandson, but as her son, too. I felt that all these years, but I never gave it much thought because I never had to. It was simple. I knew she loved me and that's all that mattered. But now it seemed a little more complicated than that. All of a sudden there was no difference between my father and me anymore; I had become him and he had become me. In her aged mind we had become one and the same. Her memory had blurred over the years, but her emotions had not. She still found a way to continue loving her son—which was through me.

When the doorbell rang it startled me. "Let's go, Aunt Marie's here," my grandmother called out as she grabbed her metal cane. All of a sudden she had a burst of energy and seemed so eager to get there. "All right…you ready? It's time to celebrate your birthday, gram!" I grabbed her arm and led her out to the car. That was the first time my grandmother actually stepped out of the house in months and even with the cane she needed help.

When we got to the restaurant everybody was there and seated already. I escorted my grandmother over to the chair with all the purple balloons tied to it. "Look what the girls did gram, and look they're your favorite color, too." "The whole family's here, everybody made it gram!" And then I mumbled to myself, except that loser Pat Cooper.

She smiled and acknowledged everybody, then slowly took her seat. One by one they all came over to wish her a Happy Birthday. Kisses were exchanged, bottles of wine were opened, and the celebration began. It reminded me of Christmas Eve except for one thing: The happiness in the room was just a façade. I saw it on each and every one of my relative's faces, and sat there wondering if my grandmother could see it, too. Everyone knew this would be her last birthday, and this was the final farewell.

When I looked at my grandmother she seemed distracted. At first I thought it was all the commotion, but then I noticed her eyes were panning the room like she was looking for somebody or something. It bothered me and made me feel sad because I knew she was looking for my father. She was always looking for him—just like me. We always thought that he would eventually come around someday. If only she knew how many times I tried to make that happen. I wanted to tell her about all the confrontations I had with him on the street. I wanted to tell her that her daughter and I just ran into him in the village only hours earlier and that he refused to even acknowledge us. Above all, I really wanted to tell her that I tried. God knows I tried; I tried for the both of us. But I could never bring myself to tell her any of that; it would have broken her heart and killed her for sure. Maybe I should have brought that picture of my father from her house. Then I could have hung on the wall somewhere close to our table, and for the first time in her life she would have felt like her son had finally come home. For me it didn't matter anymore. I lost hope a long time ago, my grandmother never did. I knew her pain all too well, but it had to be worse for her; she was a mother. And there's no bond or love stronger than that on this planet.

My grandmother was never one to look for pity—not from anybody. But if she asked me once, she asked me a hundred times. "What did I ever do to him?" And she always had the same look on her face right before she said it. I could never give her an answer because I knew she never did anything. Then one day I just answered her with the same question, "What did I ever do to him, gram? What did any of us ever do to him?" And from that day on she never asked me that question again. But that night at the restaurant I saw it coming. I saw that look on her face again and I didn't want her to go there, at least not at that moment. The last thing I needed her to do was obsess over him and miss half the party.

215

Before I knew it—it was time for dessert, which turned out to be the best part of the evening. The waiter placed the cake in front of my grandmother and me. Then to my surprise the owner dimmed all the lights and everybody in the whole restaurant, including the staff, sang the birthday song to her. It was very touching. I helped my grandmother get up into a standing position and together we blew out the candles. Everybody clapped and took pictures. Before she sat down she waved her hand like she was saying goodbye. It gave me the chills and I can still see her doing that in my minds eye. Nevertheless, it was a special moment and reassured me that my grandmother had a good time. It was a day that started out on a sour note with my father and as usual ended up on a high one with my grandmother.

After her party her health began to deteriorate very quickly. She had been swimming against the current for almost a year already, but December hit her like a tidal wave. My Aunt Marie was woken up by the nurse, in the middle of the night, and she had to rush to Brooklyn to take my grandmother to the emergency room. That went on for a few nights in a row and threw us all into a state of panic. For the first time in my life I really thought we were going to lose her, but after a short stay at the hospital and some medication she miraculously pulled through. After her release my grandmother remained despondent for days and I thought it was the culmination of things that just happened. But after I walked into her house with a huge poinsettia plant and barely got a reaction, I knew something else was up. Before I left that day I would find out.

I placed the plant down on the dining room table in the middle of all the unopened Christmas cards—another unsettling sight. I remember how she used to sow those cards together with ribbon and drape them on all the doors and along the archways around the whole room. It was a yearly ritual that I used to tease her about, and I would have given anything just to see her do that again.

After a few seconds she finally acknowledged the plant and looked up at me with a huge smile. Then she handed me her ad-

216

dress book, two boxes of cards, and asked me to fill them out. I would never refuse her, but I said, "Gram, you're not feeling well. People will understand if you don't write out Christmas cards this year." She shook her head and pushed the pen in front of me.

"Never mind...what do you think I got you for? I've done it every year and I don't plan to stop now," she said looking at me through her glasses. "Besides that's the least I can do being I'm not making the fish dinner this year."

As I sat there addressing all the envelopes she began to open her mail. One by one she read her Christmas cards to me and threw in a little story to go along with them. It was like the old days again and we spent half the afternoon doing that. We were enjoying the moment when suddenly her mood changed. She pushed a large manila envelope in front of my face and stopped what she was doing. "They're putting me in a nursing home," she said in a somber tone. I thought I was hearing things.

"Who's putting you in a nursing home?"
"The girls are."
"Gram, your daughters are not putting you in a nursing home. They never said anything to me about it."
"Open the envelope and look."
I quickly skimmed through the brochure and pictures to see what she was talking about.
"Gram, I don't even see the word nursing home mentioned in here. It's another hospital. That's what it says, and it looks better than the one you were in," I said trying to reassure her.
"Wait until you ask Marie, you'll see," she insisted.
"I'm gonna call her as soon as I get home. I promise gram, you can be sure of that! When is this supposed to happen?"
"Right after the holidays."

I left my grandmother's house completely beside myself. Why didn't my aunts tell me? That's all I kept thinking. I knew she was their mother and it was their decision, but putting her in one of those places would kill her. Why couldn't they just double-up on the nurses at the house? I had a lot of questions to ask my aunt and I was hoping that my grandmother was wrong.

When I spoke to my aunt I found out there was much truth to what my grandmother said that afternoon. She was right, but she had her wires crossed. They were putting her into a facility, except it was a hospice and not a nursing home. I didn't even know what that was until my Aunt Marie explained it to me. And when I got off the phone with her I understood it to be a hospital like I originally thought when my grandmother showed me the brochure. I felt somewhat relieved. My aunt never told me it was permanent or that it was the last place people go before they die. If I had known that I would have reacted very differently and maybe I could have done something to prevent that from happening. I guess my aunts didn't have much of a choice and assumed I knew the outcome. Nevertheless, they did what they had to do. I really thought that my grandmother would be coming home once they got her cough under control. Only God knows what I was thinking then. When I look back at it all now it was so obvious, and I should have caught on by the way my grandmother was acting. She was in rare form those last couple of weeks before she went in there. Every time I went to visit her she'd be looking around the house to give me something. If it wasn't money then it was one of those knick-knacks she had lying on the shelves all those years. Sometimes it was both. Even when I took my friend's mother there, she was giving her all her clothes. If that wasn't a sign, nothing was. It was like she was giving away souvenirs to remember her by. My grandmother was always generous—to everybody, but that particular month she was relentless. Nothing seemed valuable to her anymore. She knew once she set foot in that hospice she was not coming home. And parting with her possessions was the biggest clue and another way of saying goodbye. I can't believe I didn't see that.

Christmas Eve was always a happy and exciting time for me, a season I always looked forward to, until that year. My last and fortieth holiday with my grandmother was a sad one. The show that I thought would go on forever was over. My grandmother could no longer play the part, and the anticipation of putting her in a hospice that coming weekend was hanging over everyone's head like a big cloud. We were all pretty subdued, like never before. Even my grandmother was in a mood and we're lucky if she said two words all night. She seemed a thousand miles away and just going through the motions to make us happy.

My Aunt Marie did everything she could to emulate my grandmother and her traditional Christmas Eve dinner. She even decorated her apartment the same way and hung all her Christmas cards around the room just like my grandmother used to do. A few of the cards were sown together, too. But it didn't matter; it just wasn't the same—not for me, not for my grandmother, not for any of us. And that was because we weren't sitting at that familiar dining room table in my grandmother's house, where it all began more than half a century ago. When we were in that house, we were home, and it felt like it. We were all together, the whole family celebrating under her roof, and that's what made it Christmas. It was her show, her stage, and the place where she served us the most exciting meal of the year. That's the way she expressed herself—always. It was her favorite holiday, the one she lived for. Now, almost overnight it had become a memory like every other one. Even though it wasn't like the last thirty-nine Christmases I spent with her, I savored every single minute that night because she was still with us. And that's what really mattered.

A week later I remember it was a cold and cloudy Sunday afternoon when I first walked into the hospice. It was unimpressive and there was nothing that even vaguely resembled a homelike setting as the brochure had promised. The lobby was freezing cold and totally disorganized. There were people coming and going like it was rush hour. When I got to my grandmother's floor it wasn't much better. It was a little bit quieter, but so uncomfortably hot that I had to rip my coat off the moment I stepped off the elevator. As I hurried down the long dreary corridor looking for my grandmother's room it occurred to me that this place definitely wasn't a hospital. It looked like one and smelled like one, but it was more than obvious that nobody got out of there alive. And my grand-

219

mother wasn't going to be the exception unless some miracle happened. At first I thought she might have a chance because she didn't look as sick or as weak as the others did, but in a short time she was right up there with the rest of them.

My grandmother was not in a good mood that day and before she even uttered a word her eyes spoke to me. "I told you so," is what I got from her as soon as I stepped into the room. I felt terrible and immediately went over and kissed her pretending not to catch her look. Just as I sat down next to her two nurses came in the room followed by my aunt and uncle. I greeted my relatives as the nurses checked my grandmother's vital signs and maneuvered her into a wheelchair. Once they were done with that we took her across the hall to a larger room where we met up with more family and spent the rest of the day mingling. That's what it was like for the first couple of weeks and then she started going downhill again. She got weaker by the day and stood glued to the hospital bed for hours just staring at a television set with no sound on. And the worst part of it was nobody even bothered to come in the room and ask her if she wanted to stretch her legs. I was appalled to see her being neglected like that and knew from massage school that was the worst thing for the body. That's when I took it upon myself to walk her up and down the hallway and give her some exercise. Anything was better than nothing. I was hoping that might give her an appetite, too. When we got back to the room I proceeded to massage her feet and legs for about fifteen minutes to keep the circulation going. That was her favorite part and when I looked up at her again she'd fallen asleep with a big smile on her face. My grandmother loved being massaged and I used to practice on her all the time when I first started school.

By the end of January I was fed up with that place. I found out that they were medicating my grandmother for no reason and I was very disturbed by that. Now I knew why she had no energy to even lift her head off the pillow. When I went over to the nurses' station to inquire about the change in my grandmother's behavior they seemed aloof and looked at me like they didn't know what I was talking about. But I persisted. Finally the head nurse told me that they were giving my grandmother the standard dose of morphine to help her with the pain. When I heard that I went berserk. "What pain?" I snapped. "My grandmother is not in any pain, whatsoever, and I don't want yous to give her that stuff anymore!" I stormed away from the desk totally disgusted.

I was pissed and couldn't wait for my aunt to get there. The nerve of them and they were doing that for over a week already. I found myself pacing back and forth in the room while my grandmother sat up in that hospital bed looking stupefied. When I told my Aunt Marie she was dumbfounded and before she even took her coat off she hurried over to that desk and put a stop to it all. The next day my aunts hired a private nurse to stay with my grandmother during the night just to make sure that wouldn't happen again. I still didn't trust them. From that day on my grandmother was never the same. The little bit of exercising I had her do stopped, and she lost all desire to get out of bed anymore. I knew my grandmother was dying, that was inevitable, but those drugs made it worse and just shortened her time even more as far as I was concerned.

My grandmother didn't want to die in that place and I didn't want to see her die there either. One day while I was sitting down next to her she squeezed my hand so tightly it startled me. I didn't think she had that much strength left in her. Then out of nowhere she pleaded, "Take me out of this place! They're killin me with all this damn medicine!" I was speechless and teary-eyed. I had to look away from her. She saw my reaction and squeezed my hand again, only tighter this time. "C'mon, Mike!" she said. "I'll pay for the cab!"

Every time I think about that day I feel like I let my grandmother down. I wanted to take her home in the worst way, to fulfill her last wish, but I wimped out at the last minute. And I never stopped beating myself up over it. All because I was afraid—afraid that something terrible might happen to her in the process and afraid of pissing my aunts off. That's not to say that I didn't consider it. I weighed all the pros and cons and even looked in the closet to see if her coat was still in there. I was all ready to bundle her up and make a break for it when I realized that my aunt had her house keys. We weren't getting very far without those. Luckily my grandmother had dozed off and I hoped by the time she woke up she'd forget about the whole idea.

The last time I saw my grandmother alive was on February fifteenth. It was a Sunday. I remember I stayed at the hospice that day almost until midnight which was unusual. I always left earlier with one of my aunts just so I could get a ride home. But that night I needed to be with my grandmother alone, whether she knew I was there or not. I didn't know if I would ever get that chance again, and I was already missing those days.

I sat there wondering what she was thinking about or who she was thinking about. This was the end of the road and it was time to say goodbye. I couldn't imagine what the rest of my life would be like without my best friend around. Who would I call when I needed a laugh or when I felt like taking a trip down memory lane? We shared a lot together, but most importantly we had a common bond—a very special one. We both loved the same person and hung on to each other all those years filling the void and trying to deal with my father's rejection. That's who she had to be thinking about; I'm sure of it. I knew my grandmother all too well. She never mentioned his name while she was in the hospice, but her body language said it all, especially that last week. Every breath, every look, every gesture said: Where the hell is my son? All she wanted was to see him one last time before she died and he couldn't even do that for her.

My grandmother spent the last years of her life blaming herself and trying to figure out what went wrong between them. From all the stories I got, my father was a very needy child and a bit of a cry baby. And he still hasn't stopped crying. He craved his father's love which he never got and expected my grandmother to compensate for it. And she did. My grandmother loved him dearly, but she was unable to give him the individual attention that he needed. Her marriage was strained and they were poor from the get-go. Before my father was ten they had moved three times and in between that they lived with relatives. By the time he was a teenager his two younger sisters were born. Then a few years later my grandparents separated, which was unheard of in those days, and things only got worse. My grandfather was gone and my grandmother was left running the show. By then my father was in his late teens and the damage was already done. Every child that grows up in an unstable environment like that is affected differently—I know, and it's obvious that my father was traumatized much more than his sisters were.

The bottom line is: My grandfather was unavailable and my father, for whatever reason, didn't get what he needed to get from his mother—period! I believe this is the core of the matter and why Pat Cooper is so angry. There's no doubt he's angry for more than one reason, but the seed was definitely planted early on. That's when and where it all started and it wasn't until he got much older that all the shit hit the fan. Pent-up anger always explodes. I can totally relate to some of that, but after awhile it eats you up inside, and it's useless—except maybe not for my father; he seemed to have built a career on it. For me it's crippling, and life is too short to be carrying around that kind of baggage everyday.

My life is the perfect example of history repeating itself. My father did the same thing to me that his father did to him— shut him out. And there's nothing worse than that. It's the kiss of death, especially to a child. That's why I'll never understand, as long as I live, why my father ignored me all those years knowing firsthand what it felt like. It never made any sense to me.

When I glanced at my watch, I couldn't believe it was after eleven already. I was about to leave and when I tried to let go of my grandmother's hand it felt like she gripped it tighter. It caught me off guard because I really didn't think that she knew I was there. "It's getting late gram," I said softly. I felt another squeeze and that made me stick around. And I'm really glad I did.

I was hoping she'd open her eyes, too, and I watched her more closely just in case she did. Before I knew it I was caught up in my thoughts again and still trying to make sense of my life. But this time I felt stronger. I finally knew that I had a good foundation—one that was built on love. I was blessed to have had my grandmother around for more than forty years. A lot of people can't say that. She gave me the best part of herself—her heart, and I never had to work for it. I must have had my head up in the clouds all those years chasing my father thinking that was the only love that mattered, while all along I had the prize sitting right in front of me. I wasted so much time feeling sorry for myself that I failed to realize the thing I wanted most from my father, I was already getting from everybody else in the family. I guess things didn't turn out so bad after all. I came into this world at the right time. Everything in life is about timing, anyway. Even my grandmother was in a good place when I was born. She was still young, her house was paid off, her kids were already grown, and she had all the time in the world for me. She had other grandchildren, too, whom she loved very much, but I was the lucky one who lived right upstairs from her. My sister and I got all her attention the moment we were born, and there was also a side of her that felt sorry for us. We had no father and it was her son that messed up.

On that note, I jumped up, kissed her and left. Halfway down the hallway I got the sudden urge to go back. I realized I forgot to tell her something. When I returned the night nurse was already sitting there reading a book. I acknowledged her with a smile and she quickly sensed that I wanted to be alone with my grandmother. The moment she left the room I leaned over the hospital bed and whispered into my grandmother's ear the words I'd been meaning to say to her for the longest time: "Thanks, gram...thanks for everything!" Suddenly her hand started shaking and she slowly raised it towards my face like she wanted to caress me. I immediately grabbed onto it and firmly pressed her fingers against my cheek. I don't remember how long I kept them there; I just know I couldn't let go. I always had a problem doing that. After a couple of deep breaths I said goodbye and quickly left the room.

The next day I got up early and spent the entire morning in Central Park with my dog. I hadn't had the chance to do that in a long time and I think I benefited from it more than he did. When I got home I still had a couple of hours to kill before heading to the hospice. I wasn't in any rush that day because I knew that one of my aunts would be there to watch my grandmother.

I started to clean the house and as soon as I turned on the vacuum cleaner the telephone rang. It was almost three o'clock. I immediately thought it was my mother. She usually called everyday from work to find out how I was holding up and how my grandmother was doing.

"Hi Mom,"

"Michael, its Aunt Carol."

"Oh, hi," I chuckled. "I'm sorry I'm not there yet, but I wanted to…"

"Michael grandma passed away this afternoon,"

"I'm gonna leave very shortly, I promise. Are you gonna be there when I…"

"Grandma passed away, Michael." She interrupted a second time.

"Oh, she did," I said in a barely audible tone; then I got dead silent. I stood there frozen for a second looking down at the floor trying to hold onto some of the strength I had from the night before. When I looked up, interestingly enough, my eyes caught my grandmother's picture—the one she gave me years ago for my birthday. I tearfully smiled and silently spoke to it. "You finally got out of that place, gram. You're finally home!" I was only seconds away from breaking down when I heard my aunt call out to me.

"Michael, you still there, you okay!" I hesitated a moment then uttered, "Yeah, I'm okay." I was lying to her; I really felt like shit. She sensed that and after sharing some comforting words she told me that the rest of the family would be getting together that night at my Aunt Marie's house. She really wanted me to go, but made it clear that she'd understand

225

if I felt like being alone. Before hanging up, I assured her that I would be there.

I didn't know what to do with myself after that call. I was lost—totally lost. Now I had another void to fill and this time it wouldn't be easy. It was never easy, but I had somewhat of a life before my grandmother got sick—I really did. There were lots of things going on with me that year—good and bad. My career was peaking, my niece was about to be born, my cousin Judy had passed away, and I was in a committed relationship. While all this was happening, I was totally consumed with my grandmother and her illness. I was going a hundred miles an hour and I put everything and everyone else on hold. Then one afternoon I got a phone call and all that changed. It's like being in constant overdrive and then suddenly somebody jams on the brakes. That's the only way I can describe how it felt the moment my aunt told me that my grandmother was gone.

It would be another long and tiring week. My grandmother was laid out for three days at the same funeral parlor that my grandfather was. When I first walked in the funeral home I was standing in the lounge area for a few seconds before I heard a door open. A woman appeared and politely asked me for the family name. As soon as I said "Caputo" she quickly brought me into a larger room and escorted me all the way up to the coffin. She offered a few kinds words and then left. I stood over the casket admiring the way they had made my grandmother up. I forgot how beautiful she looked in a dress and remembered the last time I'd seen her that way was on her birthday. Suddenly everything went blurry and I realized that one of my contact lenses had fallen out. I spent the next five minutes looking for it inside the casket and on top of my grandmother's body, while all the while it was stuck to my sleeve. I immediately plopped it back into my eye, dry and all and I didn't care how much it hurt. I'll never forget how frantic I was when that happened, but now it actually seems kind of funny. I suppose I was distracted for a reason and maybe that was the way my grandmother was taking care of me from the other side.

The next three days flew and every night the funeral parlor was packed. Nothing was like that last night, though—standing room only. Everybody and anybody who knew my grandmother came to pay their last respects—everyone except her son. And the number one question in the air that night was, "Where's Patty?" Half the place was thinking that. But I knew he wasn't coming and I didn't want him to. It was too late. Besides he didn't have the guts to show up, and even if he did it might have gotten real ugly in there.

That same night one of my aunts approached me about doing the eulogy. I was honored, but I really didn't want to do it. I was so afraid of breaking down in front of my relatives and ruining it. After thinking about it for a while and realizing that this would be the last thing I could ever do for my grandmother, I quickly changed my mind. I went home and put a little outline together of the things I wanted to say. I made sure to write everything down just in case I got too emotional and lost my train of thought. I felt safer doing it that way even though I intended to speak from the heart and improvise.

The morning of the funeral was cold and dreary. As soon as I got to the funeral parlor I took my place in line and waited with everybody in front of the coffin to say my last goodbye. Then from there we would head over to the church for an hour long mass. The time had come to close the coffin and that would be it; I would never see her face again.

When my turn came I only had a few seconds. I apprehensively stepped forward and as I leaned over to kiss my grandmother's lips I whispered my final words to her, "Until we meet again!" I solemnly walked away and kept on walking until I was completely out of the room. I couldn't bear to see or even hear them close that coffin.

From the moment the priest started saying the mass I was shaking. It was freezing cold in that basement church, too, which didn't help. I couldn't believe I was having an anxiety attack over a eulogy. "You were born a nervous wreck!" is what my grand-mother would have said to me. She used to kill me with that line, but she was right. I would get the same way every time I auditioned, too. I guess that morning I was having a bit of stage fright again. There was really nothing to be afraid of and halfway through the mass I realized that I was surrounded by my loving family. With that thought in mind I felt stronger and confidently approached the lectern to give her eulogy. We are her legacy—her family. We were the most important thing in her life. There were never any re-grets—just memories and she was the master at making them.

The ten-minute ride to the cemetery was a pensive one. As we drove through the neighborhood I am saturated with memories from a happier time. I sit in the back of the limousine having flashbacks. Suddenly we've stopped in front of my grand-mother's house and for a few minutes I'm home again. I hear her in my head for the millionth time. "Look at the fancy coat I made ya, it's got a hood and all. That'll keep you warm for a long time to come! How would you like to go see your father tonight at the Copa? What would ya like for your birthday this year, Mike? You hungry—I got a surprise for ya in the kitchen. I made your favorite today. How would you like to come on a vacation with me this year? Did you remember to send your father a Fa-ther's Day card? If you behave yourself at the beach, I'll make sure to put you on a few rides before we go home. You're com-plaining, what must I say? What do ya think money grows on trees? Sure, you're a big shot with my money! Where's your hat and scarf, mister, what are ya trying to do catch pneumonia? Jesus, Mary and Joseph, you got a head like a brick! Next time you do that I'm gonna cripple ya! Listen to grandma; when you're having a bad day, Mike, do what I do; go to church and talk to God. You'll find some of your answers there. Don't ever pray for money, pray for health. When you have that you're the richest man in the world. Family and work—that's all there is! That's life in a nutshell; remember what I'm telling ya! When grandma closes her eyes one day you'll understand what I mean!"

There isn't a day that goes by that I don't think about my grandmother or her famous one-liners. It took awhile for some of the more serious stuff we spoke about to sink in. On my last visit to the cemetery, which was almost a year later, I realized another thing about her. While staring at my name on the tombstone it got me thinking; my grandfather is buried there. That said a lot about my grandmother. She still wanted to be with her husband even though they were separated for more than forty years. That's pretty amazing when you come to think of it! It showed that she never stopped loving him. It also showed that she forgave him, just like she forgave my father. One of the last conversations we had at her house was about forgiveness and she told me that I would have to learn to do that someday, too.

That day I walked away from my grandmother's grave with my head held high, feeling really good about myself. It was the same way I used to feel every time I left her house. I was finally comfortable with myself—content just being Michael Caputo and extremely proud to be one of "those people."

God Bless,
Love your son,
Michael

Made in the USA
Las Vegas, NV
28 December 2021

39704844R00141